REKINDLED HEARTS

A SPIRITUAL JOURNEY TO MARITAL HEALING

REKINDLED HEARTS

A Spiritual Journey to Marital Healing

By Doug Hinderer, MA, LMFT

Scepter

Published by Scepter Publishers, Inc.
info@scepterpublishers.org
www.scepterpublishers.org
800-322-8773
New York

Cover Image: Frank McKenna
Cover Art: DeLight Design
Text Design and Pagination: PerfecType, Nashville, TN

Paperback ISBN: 978-1-59417-539-8
eBook ISBN: 978-1-59417-540-4

Library of Congress Control Number: 2024944927

Printed in the United States of America

Contents

Preface

In the late 1970s, God first placed the desire in my heart to strengthen and help heal broken marriages when I was a psychology undergrad. But life takes many twists and turns, and it would be thirty years before I could start work on my master's degree in marriage and family therapy. At sixty, I left corporate America and launched a new career as a marriage therapist.

With thirty-five years of real-life marriage experience and a newly minted master's degree, I thought I was well prepared for the challenges that I would meet. Boy, was I wrong. The marriage dynamic was far more complicated than I had envisioned, and the challenges and problems that couples face were more difficult and nuanced than I had ever imagined. The pain, the anger, the sadness, and the loneliness were far more acute than I was prepared to address.

As I began walking with couples through their marriage struggles, one of the realizations that hit me square in the face was the universality of suffering in all marriages.

Every single marriage—the ones that book therapy sessions with me and the ones that seem perfect—contains a certain degree of suffering. For some it's just a little, for others it's a lot; but they all contain some. It was an eye-opening revelation.

No one denies the existence of suffering in life. We've all experienced physical suffering: we catch a cold, we get the flu, we stub a toe. Or perhaps we have medical problems—for example, kidney stones, which, I know from personal experience, are very painful.

In some relationships we expect suffering. We are not surprised at the difficulties at work with our boss or coworkers, with neighbors, with rude people at the grocery store, or with inconsiderate drivers on the road. But, somehow, we all expect our marriages to be exempt from suffering. Maybe it's the "happily ever after" stories we've been fed since childhood, but most of us don't expect trials in our marriage. As a therapist, I quickly learned that nothing could be further from the truth.

Catholic teaching on suffering is deeply rooted in the belief that suffering has redemptive and transformative value when united with the suffering of Christ. The *Catechism of the Catholic Church* tells us:

> Christ invites his disciples to follow him by taking up their cross in their turn . . . By his passion and death on the cross Christ has given a new meaning to suffering: it can henceforth configure us to him and unite us with his redemptive Passion.[1]

1. *Catechism of the Catholic Church*, 2nd ed. (Washington, DC: Libreria Editrice Vaticana–United States Conference of Catholic Bishops, 2000), nos. 1506, 1505.

St. Thérèse of Lisieux said, "Suffering is the very best gift He has to give us. He gives it only to His chosen friends."[2] And at another time she said, "I understood that to become a saint one had to suffer much, seek out always the most perfect thing to do, and forget oneself."[3]

Pope John Paul II's Apostolic Letter *Salvifici Doloris*, tackles the question of suffering head on. In it he says,

> In the Cross of Christ not only is the Redemption accomplished through suffering, *but also human suffering itself has been redeemed.* . . . In bringing about the Redemption through suffering, Christ *has* also *raised human suffering to the level of the Redemption.*[4]

Suffering seems to be particularly essential to the nature of man. The Pope reflects on the existential reality of suffering in human life. He suggests that suffering is inherent to human nature and is intimately intertwined with the human experience. Although he does not deal with marriage directly, his words certainly can be applied to it.

If you look at the ingredients necessary for suffering, marriage is the perfect petri dish. Suffering happens when you are treated unfairly, when you are treated unjustly, or when you are denied the love to which you're entitled as a child of God. As my wife says, in marriage we have two imperfect people who are trying to love perfectly. And that's a perfect setting for suffering. Marriage provides the context

2. Thérèse of Lisieux, *The Story of a Soul*, trans. John Clarke (Washington, DC: ICS Publications, 1996), p. 181.

3. Thérèse of Lisieux, *The Story of a Soul*, p. 67.

4. John Paul II, Apostolic Letter *Salvifici Doloris* (February 11, 1984), no. 19, Vatican website: www.vatican.va.

where the one whom you love the most often hurts you the most. Rarely intentionally, but then again, not infrequently.

We live in a society that tries to deny the existence of suffering, or at least eliminate it when it shows up. We avoid it whenever possible, and if we can't avoid it we numb it with such things as medications, drugs, alcohol, or social media. We do everything we can to escape it.

But the denial of suffering only makes it worse. We cannot avoid suffering, no matter how much we try. Therein lies the great secret of Jesus Christ, who taught us how to sanctify suffering. Of all his titles, perhaps the "Suffering Servant" is the one that most clearly sums up the life of Jesus Christ. In his message on the Third World Day of the Sick, Pope St. John Paul II said Christ did not come to remove our afflictions, but to share in them, and in taking them on, to confer upon them a salvific value: "by becoming a partaker in the human condition, with its limits and its sorrows, He redeemed it."[5] Christ taught us how to suffer and how to use that suffering to become holy.

Serious Christians reap value from suffering. Those people trying to live a life of Christian abandonment see in suffering the opportunity to unite themselves more dearly and more closely with Jesus Christ. In this union we see a path to holiness, a path to sanctity, and a path to the forgiveness of our sins. Ultimately, we see our path to heaven. Suffering then becomes not something bad to be avoided but something valuable to be embraced. It's the way we grow in virtue. It's the way we grow in our ability to love.

---

5. John Paul II, *Message of the Holy Father for the Sixth World Day of the Sick* (February 11, 1998), no. 2, Vatican website: www.vatican.va.

The challenge in our time is that we live in a disposable world. We use things and then throw them away. With the advent of "no-fault" divorce, even marriage has become disposable. We know well the statistic that half of all marriages end in divorce. But what about the half that don't end in divorce? The sad truth is that the majority of them are unhappy. God did not create marriage as a punishment (although it may seem this way at times).

And so, with all this in mind, I wrote this book not just to try to prevent divorce, although I would be very happy if it did have that effect on even one couple. I wrote this book for those couples living lives of quiet desperation in marriages that have grown stale and lifeless.

We were created by Love for love. Marriage is one of the vehicles God put in place to give us a taste of his unconditional, all-encompassing love. Marriage is an opportunity to love as God loves. It is the opportunity to grow in holiness and then to obtain the happiness that flows naturally from that holiness. I wrote this book to help people learn how to sanctify their imperfect and flawed marriages.

I may have been overly ambitious in what I've tried to accomplish. The way I see it, the book you're holding has a threefold mission.

First, I want this to be a book that can be read as you would read any spiritual book. Second, I want this to be a book that can be prayed with—a book from which you can read a paragraph or two and then stop to ponder it in Our Lord's presence. I would like you to be able to use this book to grow in your knowledge and your love of God as it pertains to your marriage. Third, I also want this to be a workbook of sorts. At the end of each chapter, I've provided you with specific ideas you can employ to strengthen your marriage—aspirations to say daily, things to read, topics to pray about, and actions to attempt.

While the specific theme of every chapter might not apply to your marriage, I guarantee there will be some nugget you can take to your prayer and apply to your marriage.

It is my hope, and was my prayer as I wrote this, that the Holy Spirit will use these pages to help you deepen your marriage, strengthen the love you have for your spouse, and see your marriage as your path to holiness.

One final word on the differences between spiritual direction and psychotherapy. Spiritual direction focuses on spiritual growth, deepening your connection with God, and living a more authentic and meaningful life aligned with God's design. Psychotherapy focuses on mental health, emotional well-being, and healing of past traumas. It addresses psychological issues, emotional challenges, and behavioral patterns. While my career focuses on the therapy side, this book focuses more on the spiritual direction angle.

There is a role for both spiritual direction and therapy in the healing and strengthening of marriages. Marriage is so foundational to human flourishing and the sanctifying of life that I encourage you to leave no stone unturned as you work to love God through loving your spouse.

CHAPTER ONE

Rose: Heaven is the Goal

Marital joy can be experienced even amid sorrow; it involves accepting that marriage is an inevitable mixture of enjoyment and struggles, tensions and repose, pain and relief, satisfactions and longings, annoyances and pleasures.

—Pope Francis

The confessional, a small wooden room that smelled faintly of incense and aged wood, was dimly lit. Fr. Richard, with his gentle eyes and serene presence, leaned slightly forward as he gave me absolution. His voice, though soft, carried the weight of authority and kindness.

"Whatever good you do and suffering you endure heal your sins, help you to grow in holiness, and reward you with eternal life. Go in peace," Fr. Richard said at the end of my confession.

"Father, do you have a few minutes to talk? My name is Rose and I've been married for sixteen years, but I'm so weighed down with sadness and have lost my sense of peace.

Even after this confession, I'm still ready to give up on my marriage and leave my husband," I sighed deeply, my shoulders slumping. "I don't know how much longer I can live with this pain and suffering."

After years away from the sacrament of reconciliation, I felt safe enough to bare my soul to this kind priest. He listened compassionately, encouraged me when I struggled to be sincere, and gave me the joy of the absolution I sought. Yet, my overwhelming tiredness and the desire to be free from my marital pain still weighed heavily on my heart. The confessional felt like a sanctuary where I could finally unload my burdens.

"Absolutely, Rose! I have all the time you need," Fr. Richard said as if there weren't several other people waiting in line for confession, and I hadn't just taken a while to unburden years of sin. His calm demeanor and unwavering focus made me feel like I had all his attention at that moment. "Tell me, what's going on in your marriage?"

"It feels like the love I once had for my spouse has been replaced with hate, or worse, indifference. I don't feel loved or appreciated. He hardly acknowledges I exist or pays any attention to me." My voice cracked as I spoke, my words hanging heavily in the air.

"When I try to tell him how I feel unloved, ignored, and taken for granted, he accuses me of constantly criticizing him, and he just shuts down and walks away. Then I get upset and lash out, saying some pretty mean things in the heat of the moment. But, you already know that since you just heard my confession."

The pain and guilt I felt from our latest blow-up had driven me to confession today. I'd been getting all the kids ready for school—hunting for lost shoes, packing lunches, loading homework into backpacks—when he came strolling into the kitchen still in his pajamas. I'd been up for over an hour, but he was starting the day late and had decided to sleep in. I was already annoyed he was home and not helping with the tedious morning routine, so when he asked why there wasn't any fresh coffee, I couldn't hold back a snide, defensive remark about how worthless he was in the kitchen. His response about not being allowed in *my* kitchen only made things worse. And then, in the blink of an eye, I was yelling, the kindergartner was crying, coffee grounds were scattered across the countertop, and he was walking away, unwilling to hear what I had to say, leaving more than one mess for me to clean up.

"I see," Fr. Richard responded. "That sounds pretty rough, and I can understand how difficult living like this every day would be. Tell me, what's your goal for this life?" he asked, his voice steady and soothing.

That was not the next question I was expecting from him. Somewhat confused, I asked, "As in, what do I want to accomplish in life? Or what legacy do I want to leave behind for my kids?" My mind began to wander, recalling my many hopes and lofty goals I had once dreamt. I had always imagined being the best wife and the most amazing mother ever. My family would be as picture-perfect as my social media feed suggested—loving, perfectly put together, high-achieving, flawless. I would be the perfect hostess and my home would be a place of comfort and rest, an oasis in the middle of a wild world for family and friends.

Today's reality looked nothing like those beautiful dreams. My husband and I argued over every little thing.

We argued about how the coffee is made and my tendency to leave the gas tank on empty. We fought about the kids' sports and even the shows we wanted to watch. It felt like we fought all the time. The house was in constant chaos and disarray, so I rarely invited friends over. I loved my children endlessly, but I was so emotionally taxed and physically exhausted that my patience was thin, even with them. My fatigue never ended.

"Bigger than that," Fr. Richard said gently. "At the end of your life, where do you want to end up?"

"Oh . . . heaven, of course," I responded, wondering if he could hear the uncertainty and disbelief in my voice. I knew that's what I wanted, but who wouldn't? At this point in my life, I wasn't sure I believed it was possible.

"Heaven! Right answer," he confirmed enthusiastically. "What's your plan to get there?"

"Plan? Do I have to have a plan to get into heaven? Can't I just live a good life, go to Mass on Sundays, and not commit any really big sins?"

I didn't remember anyone ever telling me in all my years of Catholic education that I needed a plan to get to heaven. We had the Ten Commandments, the sacraments, the Bible, the Magisterium, and the saints. Didn't they point out the way for all Christians?

"Living a good life is a beginning—a good start—but we need to go deeper and understand God's plan for your life," the good priest replied.

I didn't understand. "God has a plan for me?"

"Yep," he responded. "One specifically for you. It is in this marriage, to this specific man, that God intends you to work out your salvation. I'm not saying you shouldn't work hard on fixing your marriage. Getting help from a good marriage therapist could be a great idea, but there will always be suffering in any marriage. Even in the best marriages, suffering can't be avoided. My job, as a spiritual director, is to help you turn that suffering into the currency you will use to purchase heaven."

"I'm not sure even heaven is worth this constant suffering and heartache," I admitted, sharing something with Fr. Richard I wouldn't dare utter to another soul. "How can I endure thirty or forty more years of this? We're only sixteen years in, and the thought of tomorrow overwhelms me."

"Let's not focus on what the next forty years may bring," Fr. Richard said with a smile in his voice. "Instead, let's keep our eye on the prize: Heaven—for all eternity!"

With an almost childlike enthusiasm, he continued, "The *Catechism* tells us heaven is our deepest longing and the state of definitive happiness. Happiness forever and ever and ever. Happiness is compared to the joy of a wedding banquet and is described as paradise and peace. Happiness that will wipe away your current sufferings and trials. 'He will wipe away every tear from their eyes, and death shall be no more, neither shall there be mourning nor crying nor pain any more'" (Rv 21:4).

I let that thought sink in for a minute. After all, St. Paul told the Corinthians, "What no eye has seen, nor ear heard, nor the heart of man conceived, what God has prepared for those who love him" (1 Cor 2:9). I had to admit heaven, and all its glory, was beyond anything my limited human mind could comprehend. The saints and mystics graced with glimpses of this eternal reality were utterly incapable of describing its magnificence and grandeur.

Fr. Richard continued. "It's helpful to envision what heaven will be like. Picture your mansion, the one Christ prepared for you from the beginning of time. Imagine living in the warmth of his constant loving presence, seeing him face-to-face the way we look upon the face of a beloved friend. Think about the best day of your earthly life and multiply that by a million or so; that is what you will experience every moment forever in heaven."

"It's pretty spectacular when you think about it," I admitted.

"But here's the paradox: Heaven cannot be gained without suffering.

"Christ—perfect God and perfect man—suffered and died for our salvation. He, the Son of God, the second person of the Blessed Trinity, chose to suffer in unspeakable ways to open heaven's gates for you and me. He was mocked, belittled, abandoned, criticized, and doubted by those closest to him. Those who loved him and would later die for him left him when he needed them most.

"If he, innocent as he was, suffered all of this for our salvation, how could we be called to anything less? As St. Elizabeth Ann Seton said, 'Can you expect to go to heaven for nothing? Did not our Savior track the whole way to it with his tears and blood?'[1]

"The suffering you experience in your marriage is not meaningless or inconsequential—quite the opposite, actually. Embracing it is the very means of your salvation and,

1. *The Collected Writings of St. Elizabeth Ann Seton*, ed. Regina Bechtle and Judith Metz (Hyde Park, NY: New City Press, 2000), p. 210.

frankly, of your husband's salvation as well. It's the gold with which you will purchase eternal happiness, the path you must walk. *This* is precisely what God called you to when he put the desire for marriage in your heart, gave you the vocation, and brought your husband into your life. You committed to this when you entered into the sacrament, making vows to your husband before God.

"We need to be convinced that eternal heaven is not only worth earthly suffering but that getting there requires it. As St. Seraphim of Sarov said, 'If you knew the sweetness that awaits the sounds of the just in heaven, you would resolve to endure all sorrow, persecutions, and insults in this passing life with gratitude.'[2] Our Lord asks us to suffer," Fr. Richard finished, giving me so much to think about.

"But Father, everything you say sounds wonderful, and my head gets it. But my heart, emotionally, I don't want the pain. I just want to be happy," I told him, feeling the first flutters of hope I'd experienced in a long time.

"It will take time, but eventually, your head, heart, and soul will align. If you're serious about heaven, perhaps you'd like to begin regular spiritual direction with me," he suggested. "Are you familiar with the idea?"

"Not really," I admitted, feeling a mix of embarrassment, curiosity, and apprehension. I shifted my position, my knees feeling a little sore from kneeling for over thirty minutes.

"Here's how it works. You and I can meet regularly in my office, let's say every other week, to help you grow

2. Seraphim of Sarov, quoted in *The Spiritual Instructions of St. Seraphim of Sarov*, trans. Valery Zhakharov (Jordanville, NY: Holy Trinity Monastery Press, 1975), p. 55.

in your love of God and your abandonment to his perfect providence. Together, we'll explore your life and discover God in the middle of it. Vatican II reminded us that God is calling all of us to holiness right in the middle of the world. So, with the help of the Holy Spirit, I'll help you discover what that means in your life."

He further explained, "With me, there are four parts to spiritual direction. First, I'll give you a short aspiration to repeat throughout the day. This is to help you maintain a focused presence of God and acquire a specific virtue that will be helpful at this particular time in your life. Second, you'll try to spend fifteen minutes a day in mental prayer, and I'll give you something specific to pray about based on your spiritual needs at the time. This is really important because there can be no growth in the spiritual life without prayer. Third, I'll recommend something spiritual to read related to your current struggle. I ask you to read from that particular recommendation just ten minutes a day. You'll be surprised how much it helps. And fourth, I'll suggest something specific you can do each day to grow spiritually. This may seem a bit overwhelming, and every day won't be perfect, but little by little, if you do these things daily and we meet consistently, I believe you'll start to see and feel a change in yourself. So . . . what do you say? Are you interested?"

"I'm willing to give it a try."

"Yes!" Fr. Richard replied emphatically. "I was hoping you would say that. Does meeting every other Wednesday at 9 AM work for you?"

"I can make that work. Actually, with school drop-off, that's perfect," I told him, beginning to feel a spark of hope. Knowing I had this twice-monthly meeting was already giving me peace amid the stress I'd been feeling for months.

"Great! Any questions?" Fr. Richard asked.

"This is more than I expected from confession today. Thank you for caring."

"You're welcome, Rose! The Holy Spirit led you here today; I don't take that lightly. It's a blessing for me to work with you. It's a blessing for me to direct your soul."

"Thank you again," I told him, in disbelief that this priest was willing to spend so much time with me. I was still going back to life as it was when I stepped through the church doors, but now I felt slightly lighter and better equipped to manage the day.

"That's what I'm here for," he told me with conviction. "And Rose?"

"Yes?" I replied.

"Don't forget to do your penance so you can receive the full grace of the sacrament. Our Lord is so pleased you came here today seeking his mercy and healing. Next time, bring a notebook and let's meet in my office, but today just give me a moment to jot down your homework and pass it through the door. See you in two weeks . . ."

Go Deeper

REPEAT: "May my life be united to your holy will, my God."

PRAY: Using Psalm 84, "How lovely is thy dwelling place, O Lord of hosts!"

READ: St. Josemaría Escrivá's homily "Toward Holiness" from *Friends of God.*

DO: List the qualities your spouse possessed when you fell in love. Try to add at least one thing every day.

CHAPTER TWO

John Patrick: The Suffering Servant

Intense love does not measure. It just gives.

—St. Teresa of Calcutta

"Bless me, Father, for I have sinned . . ." I began my confession but was cut off before I could continue.

"I know that voice," Fr. Richard said from the other side of the screen. "John Patrick, it's been a while."

"Eighteen years, Father."

I had started receiving regular spiritual direction from him after graduating college and unexpectedly losing my dad in a car accident. At the time, I was lost and floundering, and he helped me correct my course. I saw him twice a month for a year before life got busy and those moments with this kind and holy priest tapered off to nothing. I never forgot him and all the good he brought to my life, but I didn't expect him to remember me, let alone recognize my voice.

"That long? What have you been up to all that time?" he asked, his tone inviting and gentle.

I chuckled. "How long do you have?"

"As much time as you need," he told me, as unhurried as I remembered him from years ago.

Taking a deep breath, I took advantage of the moment and opened up to him in a way I hadn't opened up to another person in a long time. I told him about the demanding job that pays the bills but doesn't excite me, the new house with unexpected expenses, my wife, and our three children.

"Is this the same woman you were dating back then?"

"It is. We've been married nearly seventeen years," I told him, finding it hard to believe it had been that long already.

"That's wonderful! How's it going?"

That simple question opened the floodgates—perhaps this was the reason the Holy Spirit led me here today to talk with this priest to whom I had entrusted my soul so many years ago. I needed his help and guidance yet again because the truth was my marriage was not good. I didn't think I'd even realized it had gotten this bad until I was driving home from work last night and was hit with the sudden urge to bypass the highway exit that would lead home. I wanted to leave it all behind momentarily, and my mind envisioned how much easier that option would be. I didn't follow through with the idea. Instead, I went home, fought with my wife about the latest credit card bill, then yelled at the kids when their toilet backed up and flooded the bathroom thanks to a flushed rubber ducky.

"It's hard. Really, unbelievably hard," I admitted, feeling the weight of my confession.

"Did you think it would be easy?" Fr. Richard's voice was gentle and probing, encouraging me to dig deeper.

"Not easy, but certainly not this hard. Every day is a struggle, like walking through knee-high mud. Every day, there's some new hurt, new suffering, new pain. And it's not getting better. With each year that passes, it feels like it's getting worse. I'm not completely innocent, but I feel criticized for everything I do. She makes me feel like a complete failure. Most people seem to like me. My boss and customers say nice things about me, enjoy being with me and appreciate my input, but at home, I am disrespected. And when she gets critical, she can say some mean things."

"Ouch, that can be tough." Fr. Richard paused, letting his words sink in. After a moment, he asked, "What are you doing with all that suffering?"

"Ignoring it, for the most part. I'm just keeping my head down and moving forward, working hard for my family. Trying not to think about how unhappy I am."

"And, how's that working for you?" Fr. Richard prodded gently.

"Not well, but that's all I've got now. You might remember my dad died before I got married . . . so I can't talk to him about this, and anyway, I wouldn't say my parents had a great marriage either. I don't know who to emulate or who to look at as the example of the husband I should be."

"Christ," Fr. Richard told me simply. "Christ is the example of perfect love for every married person, especially for every husband."

"I don't understand, he wasn't married," was my response.

"Ah, John Patrick, remember what we talked about all those years ago? God, in his very essence, is love. As our *Catechism* tells us, the innermost secret of God is that 'God himself is an eternal exchange of love, Father, Son and Holy Spirit, and he has destined us to share in that exchange' (no. 221). Everything he does comes from love. The Trinity is a pretty good analogy for marriage, don't you think?" he asked, his voice carrying the weight of quiet wisdom.

"I guess. I mean, I don't know, but if you say so," I said, feeling a bit cynical but willing to listen.

"You sound skeptical. Let me explain. Time and time again in human history, God reveals himself as love and shows that truth through his deeds. To Moses, he describes himself as 'abounding in steadfast love and faithfulness' (Ex 34:6). He proves it by constantly forgiving the Israelites, bringing them back under his protection, and providing for them. For this all-loving God, it wasn't enough to free his people from slavery in Egypt; he also desired to save them from their slavery to sin. God takes his deep and abiding love even further by sending his only begotten Son to redeem us. 'For God so loved the world that he gave his only Son' (Jn 3:16).

"Jesus Christ, the second person of the Blessed Trinity, does not just come and take on human nature for a handful of years while on this earth. He could have redeemed us with his mere presence. But God again proves his love, this time most profoundly and viscerally. Although blameless and without sin, Jesus takes on our sins, suffers indescribable pain, and dies. As Pope Benedict XVI wrote in *Deus Caritas Est*, 'This is love in its most radical form.'[1]

"Christ became man out of love for us, and we can learn much from that mystery. He came to suffer and to die

1. Benedict XVI, Encyclical Letter *Deus Caritas Est* (December 25, 2005), no. 12, Vatican website: www.vatican.va.

so that we might have eternal life through him. How does Christ teach us about love in this life? Through his suffering. He teaches us that love always requires self-sacrifice. Through his sorrowful passion, he teaches us that love always involves suffering. Where there is love, there is suffering; through Peter's betrayal, he teaches us how essential forgiveness is when we love; and through his loving embrace of the Father's will, he teaches us that pain and suffering are not something to be avoided at all costs but something to be embraced and redeemed. He came to earth not to eliminate suffering but to share it.

"Christ is the supreme example of what it means to love another unconditionally. He is our model of holiness—your model to emulate as a husband and a father. He sets the bar high to be sure: 'Love one another as I have loved you' (Jn 15:12). These instructions to love are not another command but rather the only response we can have to the gift of God's love, since he loved us first.

"In the day-to-day, that means you're called to love your wife in a self-sacrificing way. Consider the line from St. Paul's letter to the Ephesians, 'Husbands, love your wives, as Christ loved the church and gave himself up for her' (Eph 5:25). He loved the church by dying for her. Your lot in life is not likely to be physical death for your wife, but it does mean dying to self a little every day. It does mean renunciation and willing sacrifice. It does mean suffering and difficulties and trials. It does mean not just putting up with her defects but learning to love them as much as you love her virtues. Christ calls you to take up your cross and follow him.

"This is where the words of St. Paul from Colossians 1:24 come into play: 'Now I rejoice in my sufferings for your sake, and in my flesh I complete what is lacking in Christ's afflictions for the sake of his body, that is, the church.' We can share in Christ's suffering and participate in his work of redemption through that. This doesn't mean our suffering is pleasant or easy, but it has immense value when united with his. You can offer your struggles, your pain, your hardships in marriage as a way to share in Christ's suffering and bring grace into your life and the lives of those you love.

"Sorry, I got on a roll there, and I've given you a lot to think about . . ." Fr. Richard chuckled a little.

"But all good things!" I sighed. "You have no idea how much I needed to hear it. You haven't lost your touch." How this priest could know so much doctrine and quote the *Catechism* and the saints at the drop of a hat always fascinated me. And eighteen years later, he was still the same.

"We all need to be offered a different perspective occasionally," Fr. Richard said with the hint of a smile in his voice.

"My mind understands what you are saying, but I'm not Jesus. I can't suffer the way he did. The thought of thirty or forty more years of heartache in this marriage feels like I have an elephant sitting on my chest. I'm going to need some real help with this," I said, feeling both a sense of despair and hope. "Father, if it's OK with you, I'd like to begin regular spiritual direction with you again."

"John Patrick, I would be honored to accompany you on this journey," I was happy to hear Father reply. "You know where my office is and you know the drill. It's the same as before. I'll give you some things to think about and an aspiration to repeat throughout the day, something specific to pray about, something to read, and then something to do in the weeks between our meetings."

"I'm down for that. I still often repeat the last aspiration you gave me seventeen years ago, 'Lord, enlighten my mind and purify my will.'"

"Great!"

Our conversation had filled me with a renewed sense of purpose and direction. The path ahead seemed daunting, but with his guidance and the support of my faith, perhaps it was a journey I could endure after all.

"If it works for you, I'll add you to my calendar every other Thursday at 8 AM," Fr. Richard confirmed.

"Perfect. I can stop here on my way to work."

"It's a plan! Now, before we get to your confession, here's what I want you to do between now and then . . ."

Go Deeper

REPEAT: "Sweet Jesus, help me join my sufferings to yours."

PRAY: Meditate on Isaiah 53, the passage on the Suffering Servant.

READ: *Searching for and Maintaining Peace* by Jacques Philippe.

DO: Find at least one small act of kindness you can do for your spouse each day. Something unexpected and, if possible, unnoticed.

CHAPTER THREE

Rose: The Suffering of Christ

People who suffer have something to offer to God. When they succeed in enduring their suffering, that is a daily miracle.

—St. André Bessette

The wooden confessional was nestled in a corner of the church, but I turned down the hallway toward Fr. Richard's office, which provided a quiet, sacred space for difficult conversations and profound spiritual guidance. Fr. Richard, with his calm demeanor and compassionate eyes, sat across from me, listening intently. The light filtered through the stained-glass windows, casting a serene glow that seemed to envelop us both.

"Fr. Richard, I'm coming around to the greatness of heaven and how I want to be there," I said, my voice tinged with hope and a little frustration too. "Those spiritual activities you had me doing these past two weeks have helped."

"Good, Rose. Good. Keep focusing on the Love that awaits you in heaven," Fr. Richard replied, his voice a soothing balm to my frazzled nerves.

"What I'm struggling with now is how can I get there in a bad marriage?" I sighed heavily. "This marriage seems to bring out everything bad in me—criticism, resentment, defensiveness, cruel words, impatience, a desire to get even, and so on. These aren't the things that will bring me to heaven, so this can't be what God wants for me. How can he want me to be miserable?"

The morning's painful events replayed in my mind like an obsessive loop. My husband and I had clashed yet again; his anger was ignited by the mess of toys in the family room, the collection of breakfast bowls in the sink, and the garbage cans that weren't sitting at the curb. He blamed me for it all, never mind that the kids had caused the mess. We were still finishing breakfast, and the garbage was our eldest's responsibility. As my husband slammed the pantry door, I couldn't hold back and lashed out, suggesting that things would be better if he were around more or prioritized his family over his career. He stormed out without another word, leaving me to cry in the car as soon as I dropped off our kindergartner at school.

There's no way! I cannot repeat this type of scenario day in and day out for forty more years.

Fr. Richard's voice pulled me back to the present. "This isn't going to be easy to hear," he said gently, setting the stage for what he was about to say. "But this marriage is precisely how you'll get to heaven. When you chose your husband and made those vows, this marriage became the exact path for your sanctification. This is God's plan for you."

"So, God wants me to suffer?" I asked a bit angrily, my voice barely above a whisper.

"He wants you to live in his love and be with him forever in heaven; suffering is a necessary part of that journey. That doesn't mean you shouldn't try to fix the brokenness in your marriage. As I mentioned last time, there are many things you can do to heal the wounds, but there will always be some measure of suffering between you and your husband. In the third chapter of Genesis, God says to Eve, 'Yet your desire shall be for your husband, and he shall rule over you' (Gn 3:16). God was informing Adam and Eve that because of their sin, there would be conflict between them going forward."

"How does that make any sense?" I asked. "If God is all-loving, how can he allow me to suffer so deeply? How can I be expected to endure that?" The frustration and confusion in my voice were palpable.

"That is one of life's great mysteries, but the simple answer is you can endure suffering because Christ did it first. Of all the ways he could have chosen to redeem us, he chose suffering. That's a pretty tough mystery to wrap your mind around."

"Christ wasn't married to my spouse. He wasn't married at all," I argued, feeling anger and desperation.

"You'd be surprised how often I hear that," Fr. Richard chuckled softly. "No, he wasn't married, but he is the one you are called to imitate as a wife, mother, daughter, and friend. He, who *is* love, suffered and died for love of you, and me, and your husband. He did no wrong. He did not sin. Yet, he experienced ridicule and abandonment and loneliness and contempt. He endured physical, emotional, and psychological suffering. He could have opted for a different path. He could have stopped it. He could have snapped his fingers and opened the gates of heaven. He came not to eliminate our suffering but to join us in it.

"Christ could have redeemed us in a million different ways, but he chose to show his love through one path—suffering unto death. 'Greater love has no man than this, that a man lay down his life for his friends' (Jn 15:13). Our very salvation flows from this reality. God died so we might live forever.

"By becoming man and taking on our sin, Christ has united himself to you, making you a partner in his sacrifice. He invites you to share in his passion, take up your cross, and follow in his footsteps. 'For to this you have been called, because Christ also suffered for you, leaving you an example, that you should follow in his steps' (1 Pt 2:21).

"But this isn't just a suggested option or one among many ways to reach heaven. This is *the* way—the *only* way. As St. Rose of Lima said, 'Apart from the cross there is no other ladder by which we may get to heaven.'[1]

"Where do we encounter the cross to imitate Christ? We encounter it in dozens of small ways every day. In the words of St. Josemaría, 'That joke, that witty remark held on the tip of your tongue; the cheerful smile for those who annoy you; that silence when you're unjustly accused; your friendly conversation with people whom you find boring and tactless; the daily effort to overlook one irritating detail

---

1. Rose of Lima, quoted in *Catechism of the Catholic Church*, 2nd ed. (Vatican City: Librera Editrice Vaticana, 1997), no. 618.

or another in the persons who live with you'.[2] This saint of the ordinary is showing us the path to heaven in the middle of the world.

"In a difficult marriage, you carry his cross by . . . remaining cheerful when you have been wounded by a harsh word, smiling when you feel like crying, focusing on your husband's virtues and making excuses for his defects, and forgiving him when you want to lash out instead. Think of Christ hanging on the cross and how he asked his Father to forgive all who harmed him. Nowhere in life do we get more opportunities to forgive than in marriage.

"The critical element in all this is aligning your moments of suffering to Christ and his cross. We don't suffer just to suffer. We don't suffer just to get through it, to grin and bear it. We suffer to co-redeem with Christ. So, every time you find yourself facing the cross, lifting it on your shoulders, that is the moment to tell Christ, 'I'm picking this up with you; I'm sharing this cross with you. You must help me here; I can't do this alone," Fr. Richard concluded.

"So, you're saying that love and the cross go hand in hand?" I asked, trying to grasp the enormity of his words.

"I like to imagine that if you were talking with Christ rather than this sinful old priest, he might say something like . . ." Fr. Richard trailed off for a moment. I could see and hear the smile on his face when he continued, "'My daughter, I love your husband so much that I suffered unbelievable pain and a gruesome death to redeem his soul. I love him so much that if he were the only person on earth, I would have gladly suffered all I did just to bring him to

---

2. Josemaría Escrivá, *The Way* (Princeton, NJ: Scepter, 2001), no. 173.

heaven. Sometimes, I will ask you to suffer with me for his salvation. Are you willing to join me in the work of his redemption?"'

I didn't know how to respond, so I said nothing.

"I know this can seem overwhelmingly difficult," Fr. Richard assured me. "And, of course, it would be, without his help. But we are just beginning our journey, and he'll be with you every step of the way—lifting you, supporting you, and giving you all the grace you need for this particular trial."

The words hung in the air, their weight settling on my shoulders yet bringing a strange sense of comfort. The path ahead seemed daunting, but with Fr. Richard's guidance and the support of my faith, perhaps it was a journey I could endure after all.

"Here's what I want you to work on during these next two weeks . . ."

Go Deeper

REPEAT: "Help me to love my spouse as you do, Lord."

PRAY: Contemplate the Sorrowful Mysteries of the Rosary and how Christ calls you to imitate him in these ways.

READ: The Last Supper and Passion Narrative from John's Gospel, chapters 13–19.

DO: Find small acts of kindness you can do daily for your spouse, ideally that won't be noticed.

CHAPTER FOUR

John Patrick: Suffering as a Gift

God had one Son on earth without sin,
but never one without suffering.

—St. Augustine of Hippo

As I stepped back into the confessional, I had mixed emotions. The comforting presence of Fr. Richard always lifted me, and his warmth and love for God provided a refuge. But the complexities of my marriage loomed large, casting a shadow of fear over the future.

Over the past two weeks, I had read, thought about, and prayed with Isaiah so often that I had memorized the following lines: "He was despised and rejected by men; a man of sorrows, and acquainted with grief; as one from whom men hide their faces he was despised, and we esteemed him not" (Is 53:3). I had realized Christ's suffering was beyond description, far greater than anything I was going through.

But he is God, and I am just a man. I can't suffer like he did—not even close. I felt worse today than I had two weeks ago. I seemed more sensitive to my wife's criticisms, snapping back forcefully or angrily storming away. Maybe I was more aware of it now, but we were fighting more than ever. Not a day went by without anger and criticism. Why couldn't she just treat me with some kindness? I worried Fr. Richard would be disappointed, expecting more progress.

"Fr. Richard, I have to tell you, I'm having a tough time understanding why God would want me to endure all this suffering in my marriage. It feels like I'm being punished for something I don't deserve. I'm a good guy, a faithful Catholic. I love my kids and wife, at least I used to."

"John Patrick, why do you assume it's a punishment?" he asked simply.

"What else could it possibly be?" I retorted, frustration lacing my tone.

"To be sure, suffering and sin are connected, but do you think God the Father punished his Son by allowing him to die on the cross?"

"But that's different," I argued. "Christ died for our sins. He took on the punishment we were supposed to receive. I read Isaiah 53. I still don't understand why I have to suffer, since Jesus did it for me."

"OK," Fr. Richard said, pausing for a moment. "Let's think about this from a different perspective. Of all the human beings God created, who do you think Jesus loves the most?"

"Mary, his mother," I answered without hesitation, feeling rather proud of myself for having the answer so readily.

"I'd agree. And that answers your earlier question. Isn't it interesting that God granted Mary the grace of being born without sin? He spared her from the burden that every other human being has. And at the same time, he did not spare her from suffering. St. Alphonsus Liguori argues that no human being ever suffered more than Mary—not even close.

"If suffering is only a punishment for sin, Mary shouldn't have experienced any—she was sinless and had nothing to be punished for. If suffering was utterly contradictory to love, Mary should have never experienced it, since Christ loved his mother immensely, and she loved him completely.

"But Mary suffered even more acutely than we do because she loved more completely. Her fiat was not just a yes to being the Mother of God but a yes to everything that was entailed in the plan of salvation, including a yes to suffering with her Son. She suffered at the Presentation when Simeon foretold the agony she would later face: 'and a sword will pierce through your own soul also' (Lk 2:35). She suffered while fleeing for her Son's life to Egypt and at losing Jesus in Jerusalem. And she suffered most profoundly during the crucifixion, death, and burial of her only Son, her God.

"Maybe instead of thinking of suffering as a punishment, you can think about it as a gift from God. He gifted Mary with suffering because she could be even more aligned with her Son through it. The *Catechism* teaches us, 'There she stood, in keeping with the divine plan, enduring with her only begotten Son the intensity of his suffering, joining herself with his sacrifice in her mother's heart, and lovingly consenting to the immolation of this victim, born of her' (no. 964). Through suffering, she could join her Son in his mission to redeem all people.

"All suffering is a grace and a gift from God—whether it is part of his perfect will or his permissive will. In the words of St. Faustina, 'Suffering is a great grace; through suffering, the soul becomes like the Savior; in suffering, love becomes crystallized; the greater the suffering, the purer the love.'[1]

"Suffering gives us the chance to co-redeem with Christ. It provides us with the ability to grow in virtues. It provides us with the opportunity to prove our love through actions. As St. Josemaría Escrivá heard whispered in his heart, 'Love means deeds and not sweet words.'"[2]

I paused, absorbing his words. "I've never considered how much Mary suffered, all while Christ loved her! That's a big mental switch. I will need some time to wrap my head around that."

"It's worth pondering, especially when you see suffering as a punishment from God rather than a gift," Fr. Richard responded.

"I'm going to need to pray on this," I said, feeling a mixture of confusion and hope.

"That's the spirit," said Fr. Richard with a big smile. "Remember, as St. Paul tells the Romans, 'We know that in everything God works for good with those who love him' (Rom 8:28). It may be challenging to see right now, but good can come out of this suffering you're experiencing through your marital trials.

---

1. Faustina Kowalska, *Diary of Saint Maria Faustina Kowalska: Divine Mercy in My Soul*, trans. Teresa Bałuk-Ulewiczowa (Stockbridge, MA: Marian Press, 1987), p. 57.

2. Escrivá, *The Way*, no. 498.

"In the Old Testament, there are dozens of moments in which God brings good out of a bad situation. The jealousy that Joseph's brothers experience leads them to sell their baby brother into slavery—he must have suffered a great deal during that ordeal. But Joseph ends up in Egypt, not as a mere slave, but rather the right-hand man to Pharaoh. That position gives him the power and the resources to save his family—that same family who sold him like cattle—when famine strikes the land. He, the abandoned brother, becomes the one who ensures the line of Israel can continue.

"God took the evil his brothers committed and used it for good to save his people. He can and will do the same if you keep asking him for it and if you keep working on falling more in love with him and his will for you.

"You're doing great, John Patrick. Spiritual growth is the journey of a lifetime. Have patience, my son; you are on the right path. Have you considered finding a suitable marriage therapist to help you work through these issues with your wife? I have a couple of names I can recommend to you if you're interested."

"Let me think about that. Pouring my heart out to you in the spiritual direction is one thing, but talking about this to a total stranger is another," I responded, somewhat taken aback.

"I understand. Pray about it. See where the Holy Spirit is leading you. We can do a lot in spiritual direction, but the help and support you receive in therapy is not the same as spiritual direction. Sometimes, people need both, and there's no shame in that.

"So, here's the plan for the next two weeks: We will focus on our Blessed Mother and her life of suffering. Think about all she endured and how deeply she loved despite her immense pain. Pray to her for strength and guidance. Ask her to help you see your suffering in a new light as a way to unite more closely with Christ and his redemptive work. And for homework . . ."

Go Deeper

REPEAT: "Our Lady of Sorrows, help me to utter a resounding yes when suffering appears."

PRAY: Contemplate the Seven Sorrows of Mary.

READ: Discourse 9, "Of the Dolors of Mary," from St. Alphonsus de Liguori's *The Glories of Mary*.

DO: When small sufferings come your way during the day, say a prayer of gratitude to God, since he gave you that opportunity to co-redeem.

CHAPTER FIVE

Rose: Suffering Transforms

A new heart I will give to you, and a new spirit I will put within you; and I will take out of your flesh the heart of stone and give you a heart of flesh.

—Ezekiel 36:26

I sat before his desk, my heart a leaden weight in my chest, and before Fr. Richard could greet me I blurted out, "Father, my heart is broken—broken in an irreparable way."

"Good morning, Rose. It's good to hear your voice," Fr. Richard gently replied. "Tell me more. Why do you think your heart can't be healed?" His compassion made it easy to pour out my soul to him.

"There are so many things that hurt me I don't even know where to begin," I said, my voice cracking. "My husband's constant passive-aggressive comments and sarcasm, the way he withdraws from a conversation he doesn't want to have, the loneliness I feel when he's gone, and the even greater loneliness I feel when we're together. It's everything—it feels like everything needs to be fixed in my marriage. And this has been going on for years, getting progressively worse. How can that be undone? If I can't get him to change, I don't have any hope of ever being happy."

"I've got good news and bad news for you," Fr. Richard began, his tone both serious and reassuring. "By yourself, with your strength of will, it is impossible. But with God, all things are possible. As you work at it, God will be the one to transform your heart. Too often, we want to power through and make change happen by the force of our own will. We want to see it done—tomorrow, if not sooner—and we forget that God works miracles and transforms the human heart to look more like his on his timetable, not ours."

"But how can he do that?" I demanded as I became increasingly more frustrated. "He knows this has been going on for years, and he hasn't transformed anything in me yet."

"Don't be so sure; you're here, right?" Fr. Richard replied with a smile. "It was his grace, freely given, that got you to come to confession a month ago, and it was his grace that allowed you to unburden your soul and ask for help. He's already at work in your heart. He always has been, and always will be working in you."

I took a deep breath. "You know, you're right. I had no plans to come to confession that day. I was driving by the parish, saw the sign for confessions, and decided to stop. Something was nudging me to seek refuge in this sacrament."

"Not something. Someone! God was stirring your heart to come to him. Maybe before that, you weren't ready to give him your pain, find meaning in your suffering, and grow in your love. But you're ready now, and the Holy Spirit is leading you, opening your heart and your mind to what your vocation is asking of you."

"And will he continue to transform my heart?" I asked.

"Absolutely," Fr. Richard confirmed. "Beyond your wildest imagination! And suffering can help in that process. When we unite our sufferings to that of Christ, we can't help but be changed. As St. Josemaría wrote in *The Forge*, 'everything comes from the hands of our Father: so though the blow of the chisel may hurt our flesh, it is a sign of Love, as he smooths off our rough edges and brings us closer to perfection.'[1] The suffering you are experiencing is smoothing the edges of your battered heart.

"Let's go slow for a moment," Fr. Richard continued, speaking very deliberately. "When we suffer, we lean more heavily on God in prayer and the sacraments—the exact reason you sought confession. You probably wouldn't have come for confession that day if your heart hadn't been so heavy. For most of us, prayer of petition is the easiest and most common prayer we offer God. We remember him most when we find ourselves most in need. We call on him and ask him to accompany us or carry us through the rough waters we are treading. Suffering gives us that beautiful 'excuse' to turn to him as a young child turns to her father. She knows he will do whatever is needed to help, support, and lessen the burden. In suffering, we go to God the Father with the same request and conviction that he will not abandon us. Suffering strengthens our prayer life and, in that way, transforms the heart. Does that make sense, Rose?"

---

1. Josemaría Escrivá, *The Forge* (New York: Scepter, 1987), no. 609.

"I think so. Are you saying that this suffering I'm going through is God's invitation for me to draw closer to him and to find comfort in his tender love?"

"Correct. When we suffer, we understand just a little more clearly all that Christ had to suffer for our sins and we grow in love and appreciation for him. It's difficult to fully understand a pain we have not experienced. We can imagine it, but when we feel it personally, we know that pain to our core. Something similar could be said for the sufferings of Christ. While we will never fully understand what it means for Jesus to have suffered the pain of the crucifixion, we can understand certain elements—the betrayal of his friends, the loneliness of the cross, the humiliation of being stripped of his garments, the passive-aggressive and sarcastic words being thrown at him from the crowd.

"We can understand and unite ourselves with Christ when we experience some of that too. Your husband may never change, but when he says those hurtful things in anger, you can unite yourself to Christ when he was insulted and jeered at on the cross. Or when your husband withdraws from a discussion and walks away, you can identify more fully with the pain Christ must have experienced at being abandoned in the garden of Gethsemane and only seeing John at the foot of his cross. These daily moments of suffering you face are a chance to unite yourself with Christ's cross and co-redeem with him. Being so closely united with Christ's suffering can be a place of absolute joy if we understand it correctly.

"We can grow in patience, wisdom, kindness, humility, abandonment, forgiveness, and long-suffering when we suffer. This is a truth that the early Christians knew. In one of his letters, St. James tells the people, 'Count it all joy, my brethren, when you meet various trials, for you know that the testing of your faith produces steadfastness' (Jas 1:2–3). Imagine that! He tells the early Christians—the very people who were persecuted for their faith, thrown to the lions in the Coliseum, burned alive to light Nero's parties—that suffering should be considered pure joy. Pure joy! Why? Because it allowed them to participate in the redemption of the human race.

"When we suffer, we can empathize with and have compassion for the sorrows and sufferings of others. If we allow it, suffering expands our hearts, opening them to all people. When we know we are suffering, we are more patient, kind, and tolerant of others' defects."

"So Father are you saying that all this suffering is good for me, or God wouldn't allow it? That I can become a better, not a bitter, person because of all this pain?"

"Yes, but only if you allow it. All of these wounds will slowly work at transforming your heart into the heart of Christ. The heart of Christ that endures all things, never fails, and perseveres. Like all things connected to God, our limited intellect cannot comprehend what's happening, but suffering always accompanies love. No one loved more than Jesus, and no one ever suffered more than he did. And . . . there was no one Jesus ever loved more than his Blessed Mother, yet rather than spare her from suffering, he allowed her to participate in his suffering more fully than any human being who ever lived. There must be something incomprehensibly valuable about suffering if Jesus allowed his mother to suffer so much. In some mysterious way, suffering is tied to our redemption.

"As St. Ignatius of Loyola said, 'If God sends you many sufferings, it is a sign that he has great plans for you and certainly wants to make you a saint.'[2] God does have great plans for you and your family, Rose. For your husband, too. As Vatican II taught us, God wants to make you into a saint right here, right now in the middle of the world."

"It's hard to see that sometimes," I admitted, feeling my doubt beginning to lessen.

"God rarely lays the plan out in front of you in a crystal-clear way, but know that he has a great plan for you and is giving you the grace to accomplish that plan. He doesn't leave you to figure it out on your own. One of my favorite quotes from St. Edith Stein, a Catholic convert who died in the gas chambers at Auschwitz, is, 'I have an ever deeper and firmer belief that nothing is merely an accident when seen in the light of God, that my whole life down to the smallest details has been marked out for me in the plan of Divine Providence and has a completely coherent meaning in God's all-seeing eyes.'"[3]

"If only I had a faith like that," I sighed.

"Me too," Fr. Richard said kindly. "We're all a work in progress until we take our last breath."

"That gives me some hope," I replied, feeling a spark of light ignite in my heart like it usually did at the end of our conversations.

"That's the spirit!" Fr. Richard, exclaimed. "Now over the next two weeks, here's what I'd like you to work on . . ."

---

2. Ignatius of Loyola, quoted in Luis Gonzalez, SJ, *Memoriale Ignatius* (Rome: Jesuit Press, 1918), p. 145.

3. Edith Stein, *The Hidden Life: Essays on Personalist Theology*, trans. Waltraut Stein (Washington, DC: ICS Publications, 1990), p. 31.

Go Deeper

REPEAT: "Give me a new heart, your heart, My God."

PRAY: Psalm 21:2, "Thou hast given him his heart's desire, and hast not withheld the request of his lips."

READ: Chapter 1 from Francisco Ugarte's *From Resentment to Forgiveness.*

DO: Pick one virtue you'd like to grow in, focus on, and practice intentionally over the next two weeks.

CHAPTER SIX

John Patrick: You Are Not Alone

Fear not, for I am with you, be not dismayed, for I am your God; I will strengthen you, I will help you, I will uphold you with my victorious right hand.

—Isaiah 41:10

"Do you know what I'm finding the hardest in all of this? The feeling of being utterly alone," I confessed to Fr. Richard, my voice weary and heavy.

"Tell me more about that. Alone in what way?" he asked, gently encouraging me to continue.

"I've got no one in my corner. I can't talk about the struggles and the difficulties with my coworkers—that's not the place to unburden myself about my marriage. I have very few guy friends anymore, and the ones I have are either divorced or aren't in the kind of marriage I want. My dad's gone. My mom lives out of state and adores my wife, so I don't want to say anything to destroy that. Other than my wife, who can I talk to about this? You're the only one in my life who knows what's going on." As I explained, I felt more isolated than ever.

"How are you compensating for this loneliness?" His eyes searched mine for understanding.

"Compensating? What do you mean?" I questioned, genuinely puzzled.

"Most people, when lonely, try to fill that void with something else—something to take away the pain momentarily. It might be the company of another woman, social media, long hours in the office, alcohol, pornography, or expensive purchases. There's no end to how we combat loneliness," he explained patiently.

"I've become a workaholic," I admitted. "When I'm working, I have little time to think about the train wreck my marriage has become."

I had known for years that I was putting work ahead of my family, but it provided an easy excuse and an escape. If I didn't feel up to a battle at dinner, I worked late and got home just in time to put the kids to bed. The office had even implemented a hybrid work option so employees could work from home a few days a week, but I rushed back to full-time in the office as soon as we were allowed through the doors. And my work didn't end when I left at night. I always kept my phone on me, responding to emails at night, early in the morning, and on the weekends.

"And when you're home? Are you still working, or do you set work aside to focus on your family?" Fr. Richard asked, his voice free of judgment but seeking to understand.

At his question, I felt a deep shame wash over me. "I'm always working," I responded.

"Does your company expect that kind of commitment from you?" Fr. Richard gently probed.

"I want to say yes. But the truth is no. Many others in my position log off at the end of the day and check back in the next morning when they arrive. It's the running joke in the office that I'm the only one who is always reachable after 8 PM and even on the weekend," I admitted, now feeling the weight of my choices.

"We're going to work to change that, so your reputation becomes that of a man who works hard *and* can't wait to get home to family dinner every night. But first things first. Let's go back to the original topic—feeling alone in this struggle," he said, his eyes locking onto mine with a determination that felt both comforting and challenging.

"It's one more layer of suffering," I sighed at the exhausting thought.

"In our world today, it's a widespread sentiment for the married and unmarried," Fr. Richard added, offering a new perspective on my complaint. "And yet . . . we must remember that God is always with us even when we feel abandoned.

"It often feels like he is far away and has left us alone. That's never the case. Even before Christ came, the Israelites understood that. Think back to that famous passage from Isaiah: 'But Zion said, "The LORD has forsaken me, my Lord has forgotten me." Can a woman forget her sucking child, that she should have no compassion on the son of her womb? Even these may forget, yet I will not forget you' (Is 49:14–15). Or even the line from St. Luke, 'Are not five sparrows sold for two pennies? And not one of them is forgotten before God. Why, even the hairs of your head are all numbered. Fear not; you are of more value than many sparrows' (Lk 12:6–7). We are not forgotten, not left alone in our suffering.

"Personally, I love praying about the passages in Exodus when God leads the people out of slavery in Egypt. They are being freed from bondage, given a place better than they could have dreamt, and literally led by God through a pillar of fire by night and a pillar of cloud by day. They complain against him and don't trust that he will provide. They turn away from him and build a golden calf. And yet, again and again, God proves that he has not left them alone. He parts the Red Sea to escape Pharaoh's fury and gives them manna in the desert to eat. He gives them a simple cure for deadly snake bites and forgives their idol worship. These scenes provide a powerful testament to the lengths God goes to accompany his people.

"St. Faustina, who experienced many spiritual and physical sufferings, wrote something in her diaries that I find comforting and helpful: 'I begin my day with battle and end it with battle. As soon as I conquer one obstacle, ten more appear to take its place. But I am not worried because I know this is a time of struggle, not peace. When the burden of the battle becomes too much for me, I throw myself like a child into the arms of the heavenly Father and trust I will not perish.'[1] We can learn a lot from her

1. Kowalska, *Diary*, p. 186.

about the unending mercy and love of the Father, don't you agree?" Fr. Richard asked, his wise eyes sparkling.

"I never thought about this life being a time of struggle. Our culture is all about pleasure and avoiding pain at all costs. I guess I bought into that idea without realizing it," I admitted, feeling a sense of revelation.

"That makes sense," Fr. Richard sadly replied. "We are all a product of the world we live in. Unfortunately, the world gives us a false idea of happiness. Consider the only begotten Son of the Father, who was perfect God and perfect man. He lived among us and accompanied others when they felt alone. He stood by the woman about to be stoned for her adultery when she had no one by her side, no one coming to her defense but Christ. He restored to life the widow of Nain's only son amid the funeral procession. He healed the man with no one to dip him into the pool of Bethesda and who, for thirty-eight years, had suffered the physical and emotional pain of his paralysis and the loneliness that came with it. But then Jesus showed up, accompanied him, and healed him. Jesus talked with and eventually converted the woman at the well—a woman who needed to go to the well at that hour of the day because she was ostracized from her community because of her many husbands. If you look with new eyes, you'll find several Scripture passages in which Jesus is beside a person who feels alone. He's right there when someone needs him most.

"And the best part is that, according to St. Matthew, he promised never to leave us alone either. 'I am with you always, to the close of the age,' Matthew records Christ saying (Mt 28:20). So, you can have confidence that he's there with you every step of the way. As St. John Paul II said, 'There is no evil to be faced that Christ does not face with us. There is no enemy that Christ has not already conquered. There is no cross to bear that Christ has not already borne for us, and does not now bear with us.'"[2]

"But I don't feel him by my side like I would a friend," I responded, sharing one of the things I've always struggled with regarding friendship with Christ.

"I certainly understand that. There's a natural tendency to reduce Jesus to a feeling. Add to that the hectic, noisy world we live in, and it's no wonder we rarely know his presence in our lives.

"Remember, in the first book of Kings, Elijah's life is in danger, and he flees to the mountain where the Lord will appear to him. First, there was a strong wind, then an earthquake, and then a fire, but God was not in any of those. Finally, there was a light, silent sound, and Elijah covered his face because he was in the presence of God. That's why prayer is essential for anyone wanting to grow in holiness. It is only in the time of quiet contemplation that we can hear God and know that we are not alone. This is why prayer in front of the Blessed Sacrament is so powerful. We are actually in his presence. It is a potent, physical reminder that we are not alone.

"And let's not forget the incredible gift of the Eucharist," Fr. Richard continued, his eyes displaying a profound reverence. "The Eucharist is Christ's Real Presence among us. It's not just a symbol or a reminder; it's Jesus himself. When you receive the Eucharist, you receive Christ's body,

---

2. John Paul II, *Homily of His Holiness John Paul II, Oriole Park at Camden Yards, Baltimore* (October 8, 1995), no. 5, Vatican website: www.vatican.va.

blood, soul, and divinity. He becomes a part of you, physically, and spiritually."

I nodded, trying to grasp the depth of what he was saying.

"Think about it, John Patrick. You are never truly alone whenever you attend Mass and receive the Eucharist. Christ is there with you in the most intimate way possible. He enters your very being, bringing his grace, strength, and love. This is why the Eucharist is called our faith's 'source and summit.' It's the ultimate assurance that Christ is with us always."

A lump formed in my throat as I became deeply moved by his words. "I've always believed in the Eucharist, but I don't think I've ever thought about it like that."

"It's a profound mystery," Fr. Richard said, his voice softening. "But it's also a beautiful reality. No matter what you're facing or how alone you feel, Christ is there with you, supporting, strengthening, and loving you through it all."

As Fr. Richard's words sank in, I felt a tiny flicker of hope. The path to healing and understanding seemed more attainable, and I felt a little less lonely, knowing that I was never truly alone, especially with Christ present in the Eucharist.

"Here's the plan for the next two weeks," Fr. Richard said as he outlined my spiritual exercises with the same warmth and compassion with which he had always guided me. He jotted the plan down . . .

Go Deeper

REPEAT: "I can endure all things in him who strengthens me."

PRAY: Pray with Psalms 23, 27, 34, 63, 86.

READ: *The Practice of the Presence of God* by Brother Lawrence.

DO: Focus on the little moments when you experience God's presence in your life.

CHAPTER SEVEN

Rose: Betrayal

If you really want to love Jesus, first learn to suffer, because suffering teaches you to love.

—St. Gemma Galgani

As I hurried up the church steps, my heart felt even heavier than it did the last time I visited Fr. Richard. This week, it felt like I had taken one step forward and then been knocked ten steps back. Something was wrong—seriously wrong—in my marriage.

"I think he's having an affair," I told Fr. Richard immediately upon entering his office for spiritual direction, just needing to get it out.

"Oh, Rose, I'm so sorry. Why do you think that?" The sincere sorrow in his voice caused tears to well in my eyes. I had been carrying this suspicion with me for weeks now—carrying it alone because there was no one to tell, or at least no one who could help me navigate this properly.

"He's so secretive—more so lately than he's ever been in the past. I'll catch him on his phone when I walk into a room, and then he quickly puts it down, hiding the phone away the second he sees me. He used to spend a lot of time on his phone while at the dinner table or while we were watching a movie with the kids. Now, he's on the phone just as much, but he'll be off in the office or in the bathroom on the phone. It feels like he's hiding something. He's acting differently."

My tears now flowed freely down my cheeks. Even in the worst times over the last couple of years, I never thought he'd cheat. Never! But now . . . now I just didn't know.

"Is there anything else that has you thinking he's having an affair and not just working?" Fr. Richard asked, concerned, his brow furrowed.

"It's a dozen different things," I replied, wiping the tears away. I continued to explain my suspicions, finding it healing to unburden myself. "A couple of times now, he'll leave the house and not tell me where he's going. He'll make up some random excuse or explanation and then leave for several hours—he's never done that before. I've always known where he was—work, out for a beer with some friends, or home. There hasn't been much change in his patterns until now."

"Have you asked him about it? Tried to have a conversation about your suspicions?"

"Yes and no. I don't think I'm ready to hear that he's having an affair and that he's decided to write off our marriage entirely. I still love him, you know. I've asked where he's going or what he's up to on his phone. I called him out yesterday for hiding his phone when I walked into the bedroom after putting the kids to bed. He brushed off my concern and changed the subject. Honestly, I didn't have the energy to pursue it."

"Rose, I want to suggest a couple of practical things, and then we'll dive into the spiritual since that's my area of expertise," Fr. Richard said empathetically. He leaned forward slightly.

"Please, Father, I'm open to any advice you can give," I said, barely above a whisper.

"First, don't jump to assume an affair. A hundred different things could happen, and not all of them have to be bad. Maybe it's a difficult problem at work he doesn't want to burden you with, or a friend of his is going through a rough patch and he's trying to be there for him. It's human nature to jump to the worst possible conclusion. It's a way to protect ourselves from real danger. If we overassess the danger of a situation and it turns out there is no danger, well then, nothing is lost, but if we underassess the danger and it turns out to be a real danger, it could end badly."

"This feels bad," I confirmed, feeling a fresh wave of tears.

"And maybe it is," Fr. Richard said, not brushing off my concern. "But it might not be an affair. When we're lonely, we tend to compensate in various ways—drinking, gambling, pornography, companionship, work, or entertainment. Maybe he's fallen into one of these easy escapes. But here's the thing, Rose: you won't know for sure until you talk to him—really talk to him about it. You can jump to all the conclusions you want, you can have a million suspicions about his behavior, and you'll drive yourself crazy with the what-if game. He could be having an affair, or he could be playing solitaire on his phone. You don't know. But when you talk to him, be gentle. Do not start with an accusation or a criticism. Start with your fear. Let him know you are scared, that you love him, and are just trying to understand his behaviors."

"So, just ask him?" I asked. My emotions wavered between hope and dread. I swiped at the tears streaming down my face, upset that I'd gotten this worked up over our conversation and my fears.

"Yes, but gently. In a moment when you both have the time to talk, and you aren't feeling particularly hurt and vulnerable, and after you've asked the Holy Spirit to help you navigate the conversation, however it goes. But it's important to actually talk to him."

"And if it is awful? If it's an affair or a pornography addiction?"

"No matter the answer, together you employ the human means to get your marriage back on course—maybe therapy with a trained licensed marriage therapist, maybe something else—and you lean heavily on the spiritual means. Our Lord will love you through this."

"How?" I asked, feeling lost.

"God has been accompanying people through difficult marriages since the beginning. We know that one of the things the devil most delights in is breaking down marriages, and one of the things God most delights in is strong and holy marriages. Sr. Lúcia of Fatima wrote to Cardinal Carlo Caffarra of Bologna as he began to work on establishing the Pontifical Institute for Studies on Marriage and Family for St. John Paul II and said, 'The final battle between the Lord and the reign of Satan will be about marriage and the family.'[1] Think about it: going back to the beginning of the human race, by convincing Eve and then subsequently Adam to eat the forbidden fruit, the Great Deceiver helped wound the first marriage. He's been hell-bent on continuing that destruction ever since!

"We see marriages in the Old Testament endure many struggles—multiple wives, illegitimate children, adultery, and unfaithfulness of all sorts. But God does not abandon his children. When Abraham lacked trust in God and decided to conceive an heir through his slave, God didn't walk away. He remained faithful to Abraham and to the covenant he made with him. If anyone knows what it means to be madly in love with someone unfaithful, it's God. He saved the Israelite people, gave them every good thing, and they turned away from him again and again—both personally and collectively.

"Through the prophets, God compared the Israelites—his chosen people—to an unfaithful wife. 'As a faithless wife leaves her husband, so you have been faithless to me, O house of Israel,' wrote Jeremiah. 'Return, O faithless sons, I will heal your faithlessness' (Jer 3:20, 22). This is God's constant request to his people in the Old Testament. He is no stranger to infidelity or to accompanying his people through big mistakes. Just look at the book of Hosea. This minor prophet was instructed to marry Gomer, a woman who already had a bad reputation, and to take her back again and again when she was unfaithful to their marriage. The

1. Lúcia dos Santos, Letter to Cardinal Carlo Caffarra, quoted in Carlo Caffarra, "The Family and the Final Battle," *Inside the Vatican,* August 1, 2008.

whole book is meant to compare the infidelity of Hosea's wife to the Israelites' unfaithfulness to God.

"There is nothing new under the sun; we see the same infidelity in the New Testament and the world today. Jesus experienced firsthand the betrayal of those he called friends. Judas betrayed him with a kiss—an intimate gesture of love that betrayed three years of close companionship. Occasionally, I enjoy pondering what the friendship must have been like between them. Jesus surely knew before he selected Judas to be one of the twelve that Judas would be the one to hand him over to be killed. And surely Jesus knew that Judas was skimming money from their meager resources. And yet, when Christ mentions at the Last Supper that someone will betray him, the disciples all look confused, having no idea who he could be talking about.

"Jesus didn't treat Judas differently from the others. Clearly, he wasn't an outcast or loved any less, even though he would commit the greatest of infidelities possible. Judas wasn't the only one to betray his friendship with Christ. The other disciples left him to die on the cross with only a handful of people, mostly strangers, to offer him support and consolation. Think about that for a minute: your best friend is being murdered, and you could so easily be there with him to comfort him in his time of great need, but you run and hide away instead. Peter, the apostle Christ ordained to be the head of the Church, outright denies him three times. And he doesn't just deny being a follower; he curses and swears that he does not even know Jesus!

"You and I do the same to Jesus daily in our small actions or inactions; in those moments, he calls us closer to union with him, and we walk away or choose ourselves instead.

No matter what your husband seems to be hiding at the moment—whether it is nothing or something that appears impossible—I want you to cling to one thing: God will never leave you; he will support you through it all. Psalm 139 tells us, 'Thy right hand shall hold me' (Ps 139:10). I love this visual because it doesn't say God is far off watching what's happening or is accompanying us at a distance, unconcerned and uninterested. And he isn't even just walking or behind us as extra support—he is holding us! Holding us in the palm of his hand. No matter what our suffering is, he can say, 'I know exactly what you are going through.'"

"I could use being held right now," I admitted, finding comfort in his words.

"He'll never let go," Fr. Richard assured me, his gaze steady and reassuring.

"I'm not sure our marriage can survive an affair. Or maybe, more accurately, I don't know if I can survive it." My voice trembled, betraying my fears.

"Can I tell you something that isn't going to be easy to hear?" Fr. Richard asked, his tone serious but gentle.

"I trust you, Father," I said quietly.

"As Christians, we are called to radical forgiveness. In fact, our salvation depends on it. Think about it: each time we pray the Our Father, we ask God to forgive us to the measure with which we forgive others. We are constantly unfaithful to him and his commandments, and we are asking him to forgive those moments in the same way that we offer forgiveness to others. It's a radical teaching. In Matthew's Gospel 6:14–15, immediately after teaching the apostles the Our Father, Jesus says, 'If you forgive men their trespasses, your heavenly Father will also forgive you; but if you do not forgive men their trespasses, neither will your Father forgive your trespasses.' That's a pretty scary thought."

"I don't know how I would even begin to forgive him if he's having an affair with another woman, even if it is just an emotional affair," I confessed, feeling a fresh wave of tears wash over me.

"Ask the Holy Spirit. He will work in your heart and give you the grace you need to offer forgiveness—whether your husband actually asks for it or not. And it won't be the work of a single moment or a single decision. Forgiveness takes work and time. But we might be jumping way ahead of ourselves here. Go home, plan a date, talk to your husband, and trust that no matter his response, God will be holding you in his hand the whole time."

"Thank you, Fr. Richard, I will try." I was beginning to feel hopeful despite the overwhelming uncertainty about what could be going on with my husband.

"And know I'll be praying for you too. Before you come again, here's your homework . . ."

Go Deeper

REPEAT: "Deliver me, O Lord, from the fear of being wronged."

PRAY: Consider the relationship Jesus had with Judas.

READ: Chapter 4 from Francisco Ugarte's *From Resentment to Forgiveness*.

DO: Control your imagination about what might be going on and gently dialogue with your spouse.

CHAPTER EIGHT

John Patrick: Anxiety

The Cross will not crush you; if its weight makes you stagger, its power will also sustain you.

—St. Padre Pio of Pietrelcina

"John Patrick, how has it been trying not to compensate for your difficult marriage by filling the time with work?" Fr. Richard asked me, diving straight into the heart of the matter without any small talk.

Fr. Richard's warmth and love for God created a haven for me to be vulnerable and honest. Over the last two weeks, I had been trying to set better boundaries regarding work—leaving the office when most of my coworkers did, keeping my phone away from the dinner table, and putting it down when my wife or kids walked into the room so I could focus entirely on them.

"It's not been easy, but I'm making some progress. I realized after we talked last time that you were right. I caught myself reaching for my phone as a distraction and a way to feel useful and needed anytime life felt difficult at home. Each time my wife started talking about her worries or concerns, I had this urge to grab my phone and escape."

"Noticing these tendencies is a good first step. What do you do when you recognize the urge?" Fr. Richard asked, encouraging me to continue.

"I try to resist it. I tell myself to put the phone down and focus on what she's saying; that work will still be there in a few minutes." It could be frustrating at times, but I was still determined to keep trying.

"That's good, John Patrick. I want to encourage you to take that inner monologue one step further and turn it into an inner dialogue—with God. Next time you want to reach for your phone, remember what we talked about last time and how St. Faustina would throw herself into the arms of the Father. You can do the same and ask him to be your support."

"That's good. I never thought about turning to God in those moments. I've been trying to muscle through," I admitted, a little ashamed that I hadn't thought of that myself.

"Yeah, that muscling through strategy doesn't usually work. It tricks us into assuming we are strong enough to do the work independently without Our Lord's help. St. Augustine said, 'Without God, we cannot; without us, God will not.'[1] He waits for you to ask because, like a weak child, we need our Father. But he is always ready to give you what you need," Fr. Richard said, his voice filled with gentle wisdom.

---

1. Augustine of Hippo, *Enchiridion on Faith, Hope, and Love*, trans. Bruce Harbert (New York: New City Press, 1996), p. 9.

"Can he help me deal with my wife's anxiety? She's worried about everything, always assuming things will turn out horribly, and I'm beginning to feel it rub off on me. A couple of days ago, my boss called me into the office to talk, and for the first time, I worried it would be a difficult conversation. In the past, even when I knew it would be challenging, I also knew I'd get through it. But her constant worry is taking a toll on me and her too, I'm sure.

"Just last week, with the tragic news of another school shooting, my wife had to be convinced to send the kids to school. She didn't want them to get on the bus in the morning. She started looking into homeschooling and what that would entail for her. She asked the kids multiple times a day if they knew what to do in an emergency, if they could identify the exits in each of the rooms at school, and if they were rerunning active shooter drills. It was exhausting for the kids and me. Our oldest started crying at the dinner table after a week of constantly worried questions from my wife.

"Any ideas on how I should be helping her with her anxiety?" I asked, somewhat desperately.

"Sure, first, don't try to fix her, but pray for her. Pray that she can find the peace of Christ. Pray that the Holy Spirit will give her his peace. And concretely, you can be her safe harbor in the mental storms she encounters. She needs to know that you will be there to listen to her worries, acknowledge her valid concerns, and protect her as you can," Fr. Richard said, his words resonating deeply.

"I like the idea of being her safe harbor, although I'm not sure she'll feel that from me. I'm probably one of her greatest sources of anxiety," I admitted guiltily.

"That's possible. But you'll gain her trust by listening—seeking to understand, not to change or fix her. Your listening should be characterized by empathy. She needs to hear you tell her she's right to feel how she feels and that you would feel the same if you were in that situation. You need to affirm her heart and character as good and beautiful. You must acknowledge and praise her as one of God's greatest creations. It will take time, but she will eventually trust that you can be that safe harbor for her in these storms," Fr. Richard advised, his tone filled with gentle encouragement.

"I'll try." His words ignited a spark of hope.

"Good, John Patrick, good! God is pleased with our attempts, as meager as they are at times. One more idea you may find helpful. Make a list of all of your wife's qualities and virtues. Write down all the attributes she possesses that you are grateful for. What are the things about her you want to thank God for? And then share with her one of those gratitudes each day for the next two weeks."

"Those are some great ideas, and I'll admit I haven't thought much about her good qualities or virtues in quite some time. But I will really try to put your suggestions into practice when I get home this afternoon," I said, feeling a sense of purpose.

"Beautiful. Now, let's talk about *your* worries. Anxiety is such a common emotion today, and at times, it might seem like this is new to us, that we have so much more to be anxious and worried about than the previous generations did. But we see Christ talking about anxiety multiple times in the Gospels. We see the psalmist, who wrote centuries before the birth of Christ, addressing it. For instance, Psalm 37:7 states, 'Be still before the LORD, and wait patiently for him; fret not yourself over him who prospers in his way, over the man who carries out evil devices!' And we see Jesus experiencing anxiety firsthand in the Garden of Gethsemane.

"This is a reality for humankind. A reality that God can help us navigate. For me, three Gospel passages stand out when we look at anxiety and what our response should be. The first is Jesus during his agony in the garden, the second is the Upper Room after the Resurrection, and the third is the household of Martha, Mary, and Lazarus. Will you allow me to explore each briefly?" he asked, his eyes twinkling enthusiastically.

"Father, I'm all ears. I've never even considered that Jesus also suffered from anxiety," I replied, intrigued.

"In his human nature, he did. We read in the Synoptic Gospels that while in the Garden of Gethsemane after the Last Supper, Jesus says, 'My soul is very sorrowful, even to death' (Mk 14:34, Mt 26:38). Some translations of this passage have it written as his soul is "anxious." We see this isn't just Jesus expressing an emotion. His anxiety about what was to come permeates his whole body. St. Luke told us, 'His sweat became like great drops of blood falling down upon the ground' (Lk 22:44). This isn't artistic license on the part of the Evangelist to try and communicate what Christ was feeling. This is a natural phenomenon that can happen in moments of extreme anxiety.

"That Jesus experienced anxiety before his death—which was the whole reason for his existence on earth—should tell us something about anxiety in our own lives. It will happen. His response to the anxiety is even more telling. He doesn't wallow in it. He doesn't allow the anxiety to hold him back. He doesn't pretend not to be experiencing it.

He doesn't do any of that. Instead, he turns to the Father in prayer. Again and again and again. He asks that the upcoming suffering be removed if it is the will of the Father. The Father's answer is no, the passion will happen because it is essential for the salvation of all mankind. But St. Luke also tells us that Jesus was sent an angel who strengthened him. Prayer and abandonment to the will of God are the antidote to anxiety.

"God the Father will do the same for you and for your wife. When you find yourself anxious, follow the example of Christ. Ask for relief, tell God you want to align yourself to his will, and then ask for the strength to handle whatever his response happens to be.

"God will not leave you alone. We see this, too, when Jesus visits his apostles after the Resurrection. He comes to them while they are hiding away in the Upper Room. Like cowards, they didn't accompany him to his death, and now, like cowards, they are hiding rather than sharing Christ's message with the world. Jesus appears, seemingly out of nowhere. He walks through a locked door, and what's the very first thing he says to them? 'Peace!'

"I'm sure you can imagine the level of anxiety the apostles were experiencing in those moments. They were afraid of the angry mob that might carry them away to be crucified like Christ. They were probably disappointed in themselves for leaving Jesus alone and doubting his words that he was, in fact, the Messiah. And then Jesus is standing in front of them—wounds and all. Put yourself in their shoes. That would stress me out.

"But Jesus doesn't want them to live in a constant state of stress and anxiety. He wants them to have peace! He tells them this and that he is giving them his peace. And then, to further his message of peace, he gives them the Holy Spirit, who offers gifts that bring peace.

"I'm sure there were many other moments when the apostles felt anxious, even after Pentecost. But they had the gifts of the Holy Spirit, and they could remember Christ's words to them when they were at their lowest. They could lean on the Holy Spirit to help them navigate their anxiety and refine their perspective.

"You and I can do the same. There will be moments for all of us when the worries of the world and the stresses of the day take up residence in our heads and hearts. There may be moments when these concerns feel insurmountable. But Jesus has given us his peace, and he wants us to live in a state of inner calm—not a state of stress. Jesus himself has given us an example of how to live this. When anxiety arises in us, we should turn to our Father, God, and ask him for the support we need. In your daily prayer time, turn your worries over to Our Lord. He can handle them for you," Fr. Richard concluded with great conviction.

"OK, got it. What about the passage of Martha and Mary you mentioned?" I asked, eager to hear more.

"Why don't you use that scene for your prayer this week?" Fr. Richard suggested with a knowing smile.

"Sounds good," I agreed, feeling a sense of anticipation.

"Here's the plan for the next two weeks." Fr. Richard began to outline my spiritual exercises . . .

Go Deeper

REPEAT: "Help me be her safe harbor."

PRAY: Consider Martha and Mary from Luke 10:38–42. Plus, turn your worries over to God and ask him to give you his peace.

READ: *Trustful Surrender to Divine Providence* by Fr. Jean Baptiste Saint-Jure.

DO: Be patient, understanding, and reassuring of your spouse's concerns. Make a list of your spouse's great qualities and share them. Pray for peace for both of you.

CHAPTER NINE

Rose: Withdrawal

My soul clings to thee; thy right hand upholds me.

—Psalm 63:8

"Fr. Richard, it has been a tough two weeks," I said, heavy with exhaustion and frustration as I settled into my usual chair across from his large mahogany desk.

"Did you have that difficult conversation and confirm your suspicions that he's having an affair?" Fr. Richard's voice was calm, but his concern was evident.

I sighed deeply, feeling the weight of the past weeks pressing down on me. "I tried—multiple times! But he brushed me off every time I brought it up and sometimes just walked away during our conversation. He doesn't want to talk about what's going on. He doesn't want to hear that I think both he and our marriage need work."

"And what did you do when he would walk away?" Fr. Richard asked, leaning forward slightly.

I laughed a little, a humorless sound that echoed my frustration. "I'd walk after him and try to keep talking. I followed him into the garage once, out into the yard another time. But he wouldn't maintain the conversation and kept withdrawing from me physically and mentally."

The weekend memories came rushing back, and I felt my heart ache anew. "This weekend was particularly challenging. I had finally gotten up the nerve to suggest a date so we could talk and I could air my suspicions. But when I asked him about getting a babysitter to have dinner and talk, he asked what I wanted to discuss and questioned why we couldn't talk now. That turned into an argument, with me pushing for the date night and him wanting specifics of the conversation I planned to have. In a moment of anger, I told him he never gave me what I needed, and I never asked anything of him. He looked incredulous at the mere suggestion he doesn't provide, pointing out the long hours he works to do just that. He brought up work, and I latched onto that, complaining about the long hours and his constant need to be on his phone. He brushed that off too."

I paused, the pain of the next part almost too much to bear. "And then I snapped and accused him of cheating during all those long hours away. His only response to that heated declaration was to say I was paranoid and he'd never cheat. My comment about him having an affair made him angry, and he just turned and walked away. I followed him through the kitchen, the family room, the laundry room, and then out into the backyard, continuing to talk with the hopes that he would say something to prove my suspicions wrong—other than his flat-out denial. But he wouldn't talk about it anymore. He said nothing and focused all his attention on cleaning the grill. I was so angry and so hurt and pretty scared as well, I guess."

Fr. Richard listened patiently, his expression thoughtful. "Do you know what a man's greatest need is? And his greatest fear?"

"No, I've never really thought about it," I admitted, slightly confused but curious about where he was leading.

"Psychology tells us, and not surprisingly, the Bible backs this up, that a man's greatest need is to be respected, and his greatest fear is failure. Conversely, a woman's greatest need is to be loved, and her greatest fear is abandonment. St. Paul writes about this to the Ephesians: 'Let each one of you love his wife as himself, and let the wife see that she respects her husband' (Eph 5:33). This wasn't him saying women are second-class citizens; he wisely pointed out a true reality in our gender differences. Even after the first sin in the Garden of Eden, God warns Adam and Eve that they will now experience strife in their marriage, and what did he tell them that strife will look like? 'Your desire shall be for your husband,' in other words you'll want him to love you, and also 'he shall rule over you,' meaning he will do what needs to be done to feel respected (Gn 3:16). The original sin of Adam and Eve resulted in conflict over power and control for all marriages until the end of time. Husbands and wives will struggle with the question of 'who's in charge around here' throughout their entire marriage.

"So, your attempt at a difficult discussion that spiraled into a fight and your chasing after your husband plays into both these fears and these wants. He probably perceived your commentary as suggesting he's failing as a provider—an internal fear of his, even if he's never voiced it. And by your pointing it out, he felt disrespected. Conversely, you fear abandonment, so when he walks away, your automatic response is to follow, and since you need love, you keep trying to engage him. For many couples, it can be a complicated cycle that causes a lot of hurt. The psychologists refer to this as a pursue/withdraw cycle, and it is very common."

"This happens all the time in our marriage. All the time!" I said as the realization struck me.

"It happens all the time in a lot of marriages, and some of the time even in really good marriages," Fr. Richard explained, his words bringing me a measure of peace. It helped to know that our struggles were not unique.

"So, do I just stop chasing him? Let him walk away and live with these feelings of rejection, abandonment, and lack of love?" I asked, feeling torn and uncertain.

"Yes . . . and no," he said with a slight chuckle. "Yes, there are going to be times—most of the time—when you should not chase after him to keep the conversation going. Give him time to think about your concerns; hopefully, he will return to you when he isn't being called out and humiliated. This might be a good time to acknowledge he isn't comfortable talking about this topic right now and ask him when he would be willing to get together. But there will be times when you need to push for a conversation. Obviously, a good marriage requires open communication between both of the partners. This will not happen when you are both heated and upset. Step away, give him time, give yourself space to calm down, and then return to the conversation when you are both ready. In the meantime, since you need to feel loved and fear abandonment, not pursuing him might feel exactly the opposite of what you crave.

Take advantage of this moment and consider how your husband loves and cares for you. Consider the good traits and the things you fell in love with and still love today. Can you think of anything?"

Thoughts swirled through my mind. A mixture of all the things I wished he did but didn't, and then, slowly, the things he did do for me. "This will sound insignificant, but he's always ensuring I have a full gas tank."

"That's beautiful and not insignificant. He's showing his profound love for you by making sure you are never in a situation where you'll be stranded—alone or with the children—without gas. He's providing for you and protecting you. Two of his most important jobs as a husband."

"I'm not sure I'll be able to think of all these things when in the heat of the moment. Instead, my mind starts running through all the things he doesn't do, all the ways I don't feel loved, all the times he's walked away when I needed him to stay," I admitted.

"Of course, that makes sense. You have fallen into what psychologist John Gottman calls a Negative Sentiment Override.[1] When hurt, we focus only on the negatives and fail to see the positives. The Greek word for this is *scotoma*, which means blind spot. We develop a blind spot to our spouse's positive qualities and only see the defects. This is a cancer to a marriage, not to mention it gives a very unbalanced view of your spouse. So, these are the moments when you turn to Our Lord. He will never abandon you; he

1. John Gottman and Nan Silver, *The Seven Principles for Making Marriage Work* (New York: Harmony Books, 1999), p. 23.

always shows love for you and knows abandonment first-hand. He can be the one you lean on in these moments."

"How so?" I asked, needing to understand more.

"There are many times in the Gospel when we see Jesus pouring out his love for his followers, and they choose to abandon him instead. They withdraw and walk with him no more. Think of the Eucharistic discourse when Jesus explains to them the revolutionary plan of him remaining with them always—body, blood, soul, and divinity, really truly and substantially—in the appearance of bread. For many, this sounded crazy and difficult to comprehend or accept. And so, St. John tells us, 'After this many of his disciples drew back and no longer went about with him' (Jn 6:66). You'll notice here John points out that these were disciples. These weren't just bystanders who happened to catch one isolated time Jesus was teaching a crowd. Those who left were people who walked with him from town to town. They saw him curing every ailment, forgiving sins, and working miracles. They knew the sort of person Jesus was. They knew, from experience, that he wasn't a liar or someone prone to wild exaggerations. And yet, they left.

"And do you know what Jesus doesn't do? He doesn't chase after them. He doesn't try to convince them to stay. He doesn't change his doctrine to make it more palatable. Why? Perhaps because he was rooted in the Father's love for him and the truth, so he didn't have to chase.

"One of the passages I love to consider the most when it comes to abandonment is that of the Rich Young Man. I'm sure you know the story. A young man who lives a good and upright life approaches Jesus and asks him what he needs to do to obtain eternal life. It's a beautiful and profound question we should all be asking. And the Gospel says at that question, 'Jesus looking upon him loved him' (Mk 10:21). What must that gaze have been like? The King of the whole universe, the God who knows us intimately, the person who died for the salvation of every soul for all of time, looks at you with such a profound gaze that, as an observer, St. Mark could feel the love. It must have been staggering and so beautiful.

"With love, Jesus tells the young man what he has to do—sell all he owns and follow him. And what happens? After that loving look—eye to eye with the master—he walks away, for he had many possessions. What a blow to Our Lord that this man would, after living a good and upright life, so quickly turn away from the person who would bring him ultimate happiness. He abandoned Jesus.

"And it goes almost without saying that Jesus is abandoned by his disciples as he dies on the cross. Peter abandons him through his three-time denial. He is abandoned at the Garden of Gethsemane when Peter, James, and John cannot even remain awake while he agonizes over what's to come. As he is being led to his death, carrying the cross of our salvation, he is abandoned by the people of Jerusalem—the same people who greeted him like the reigning king just days before.

"So, Rose, when you feel abandoned, you are in good company. Lean on Christ in those moments. He will console you and comfort you. He will teach you by his life how to respond. And he will give you the grace you need in the moment," Fr. Richard concluded.

"I've heard the story of the Rich Young Man hundreds of times in my life, and I have to admit I've always considered the story from his perspective and thought of him as foolish for walking away from the greatness of God. But I've never considered the story from the perspective of Jesus."

"Looking at the Gospel passages from this perspective can give you many new insights into who Our Lord is and how much he's done for you out of love."

"I will try it with some of my other favorite passages. So, what do I work on during these next two weeks?" I asked, feeling a renewed sense of purpose and hope.

"Great question . . ."

Go Deeper

REPEAT: "Help me turn to you, Lord. You who will never abandon me."

PRAY: Consider the Garden of Gethsemane and Christ finding his apostles asleep three times.

READ: *A Man Who Knew How to Forgive* by Francesc Faus.

DO: Don't chase your spouse. Appreciate and accept your spouse's limitations, and look for the little things that show your spouse's love.

CHAPTER TEN

John Patrick: Criticism

It's hard!—Yes, I know. But, forward! No one will be rewarded—and what a reward!—except those who fight bravely.

—St. Josemaría Escrivá

I was five minutes late walking into spiritual direction that week because it was difficult to get out of the house with the kids all home for spring break. I was winded and discombobulated when I finally entered the church doors.

"Sorry I'm late, Father. Today has been a disaster since before I woke up," I told him, trying to catch my breath.

"In what way?" Fr. Richard asked, his voice calm and welcoming.

"I had to work late last night to hit a work deadline, so I decided to sleep in a little this morning to compensate for the lack of sleep. When I finally reached the kitchen at 7:30, the kitchen was a disaster, and my wife was not happy—to say the least."

"Sounds like there is a story there," he prompted, leaning forward with interest.

I chuckled a little, thinking back on it now. "The kids are on spring break this week. But I guess they woke up early and decided to make pancakes on their own. But not just any pancakes—some deluxe chocolate candy concoction they made up, which required most of the cooking supplies. My wife came down in the middle of them drizzling chocolate syrup onto the frying pan, hoping it would act like butter. She yelled, which startled them. Suddenly, chocolate chips were all over the floor, pancake batter was dripping down the cabinets, and chocolate syrup was all over the stove. Then I showed up, after she had just finished cleaning everything, and asked why the coffee wasn't made."

Fr. Richard was laughing by the time I finished retelling the story. "I imagine that didn't go over well."

"Probably the worst thing I could have said. She then tore into me about how I'm never around to help with the kids, and I leave her to do all the work. I defended myself, and suddenly she brought up my parenting failures from when our first child was a baby, which quickly escalated to her stating that I was a horrible father."

"That must have been difficult to hear," he said compassionately, no longer laughing.

I nodded in agreement. It was painful. It cut pretty deep. "I try hard to be a good father, to provide for them, to give them a great home, and to give them my attention when I'm around. I think it was especially tough to hear since I've been working at being more present with her and the kids. What she said made me feel like all my efforts these last weeks have been worthless."

"They aren't worthless in the eyes of God—and those are the eyes that truly matter."

"I know that, but how do I get over her constant personal criticisms? It feels like every time I turn around, she's got something negative to say—usually about the smallest, stupidest things. She complains about how I drive, the shows I like to watch, how I interact with the kids, and how much time I spend at work. Hell, she complained the other day about how I brush my teeth!"

Fr. Richard honestly laughed at this. "How do you brush your teeth?" he asked between breaths.

I laughed, too. "The same way everyone else does. She thinks I press too hard and am ruining brushes too quickly."

"Criticism can be hard for anyone to take, but it is especially challenging for men. When we are criticized, it hits at our deepest fear—that of being a failure. So, it's no wonder that when your wife said you aren't a good father, you were deeply wounded. Add to that that you have been intentionally working on being more present, even if she doesn't know that, and there you have a recipe for feeling a lot of pain. How did you respond?"

"I lost it and blew up, yelling to defend myself, and then walked away, claiming I needed to get some work done in the office. She didn't like that much either," I admitted, feeling like I utterly failed this morning.

"I can imagine that was hard for her. It looks like you will need to send an apology her way. Are you ready for some difficult truths this week?" Fr. Richard asked, his eyes searching mine.

"I'm always open to what you have to say," I replied, bracing myself.

"Here goes . . . when you are criticized, whether by your wife, your boss, maybe even your kids, remember Christ too faced harsh criticism in his day. Christ and his Church face criticism still today! Think of his passion and death. It was full of moments in which the people around him were critical of who he was, what he said, and his power. The soldiers blindfolded him and began to hit him, telling him to prophesy as to who was hitting him. He was called a blasphemer for speaking the truth."

Fr. Richard paused, letting his words sink in, and I nodded as I grasped their meaning.

"When Christ was nailed to the cross, suffering all that he could for love of you and me, he had people shouting critically at him. They said, 'He saved others; he cannot save himself,' and 'Let the Christ, the King of Israel, come down now from the cross' (Mk 15:31–32). Could he have done that? Absolutely. Were their words fair or just? Not at all. But Christ took these moments of harsh criticism. He didn't argue with them. He didn't try to explain why they were wrong or misinformed. He accepted the criticism sent his way and gave himself entirely for their salvation. And why did he tolerate the contempt? Because that was the path to redemption."

Fr. Richard's words hit me hard. I had never thought about criticism in this light before.

"Or we can go back even further and look at Moses in the desert. There, he worked amazing miracles in front of the Israelites. He led them out of Egypt and saved them from Pharoah's wrath. But what did the people do? Complain—a lot! They went so far as to say it would be better for them to have remained slaves in Egypt. They had no food. Moses prayed. God sent manna to feed them. And the people were critical because they wanted something more, something better. So then God sent quail. And still, they were not happy. So, when you are being criticized, remember you are in good company!"

"So just grin and bear it?" I asked, not sure I'd be able to do that successfully dozens of times a day.

"In part, yes. But I want something more for you than just muscling through the criticism she throws. Align your suffering with that of Christ. Offer those harsh words, those feelings of failure to God for your spouse, for your children, for your marriage. Give it to him and let him work the miracles. Start your morning on your knees and offer all your trials, pains, and sufferings to God for the healing of your marriage.

"And remember, when you took those marriage vows, it wasn't you promising to love your spouse only when it was easy, or only when there was no suffering. No. You vowed to love her in good times and in bad ones. You vowed to love her when she doesn't love you how you want or need to be loved. You promised her, and God, that you would love her to the point of suffering as Christ did for us."

"I did make that vow. And I meant it at the time. I just didn't think it would be this difficult," I told him honestly.

"Nobody does! Admittedly, on your own, you wouldn't be able to endure all of the suffering that marriage often entails. But you aren't alone! You are a beloved son of God. Let that thought settle in for a while. He is with you always and gives you the grace you need to get through any situation you encounter. He's got your back—always."

"That truth is giving me a lot of strength these days."

"Good! Pray about it often. Our identity as a child of God is too often overlooked or ignored, but it informs everything!"

"So, should I not talk to my wife about all these things she is critical of?"

"Not at all. Just because Christ didn't say anything to those criticizing him on the cross doesn't mean there isn't a time and a place to have that discussion. I'd suggest waiting for a day when you aren't feeling like a failure, and she isn't too critical, and then having a good heart-to-heart conversation. One of the best formulas I've come across for having these challenging talks with a loved one goes like this: Begin by saying 'I feel' and then fill in the emotion you are experiencing. Next, offer what she does that makes you feel this way by saying, 'When you . . .' And then you end with, 'So I'd like to ask you to please . . .' and point out the different reaction you'd like to see.

"So, in your case, it might sound a little like this: I feel. . . like a failure as a husband and father when you . . . point out things I'm not doing for the kids. I'd like to ask you to please . . . mention those things in a kinder tone to help me see how I can love them better."

"I like this formula. It's easy to remember and hopefully easy for me to use."

"The key is not to be defensive when you have the conversation and to not be critical in turn. You are pointing out your valid emotions when she does something and suggesting a way to approach the situation differently. It's a very gentle way to begin a conversation, and from my experience, it can lead to some very profound conversations that might not have happened otherwise. Perhaps you can take your wife out on a date, maybe dinner at a nice restaurant, and you can talk gently with her about what you are feeling. One word of caution: be prepared for her to share some of the hurt she is experiencing. You need to accept her pain without getting defensive."

"I wrote the formula down so I can start practicing it this week," I said with a renewed sense of hope.

"Excellent. One more question before I let you go."

"I'm all ears!" I replied.

"How did you do with the suggestion I made the last time we met to list all the things you love about your spouse—all her gifts, talents, and strengths? Did you thank God for her virtues and look for ways to compliment her on these items, and do this daily?"

"I made a list of the things I love about her and was surprised about how many points I came up with, but I didn't do a very good job of praising her on those qualities," I admitted.

"You might find that by looking for moments to compliment her, she is less critical of you. St. John of the Cross has this great quote that I think of often: 'Where there is no love, put love—and you will find love.'"[1]

"I can do that!" I said, feeling inspired.

"That's the spirit! Now for the next two weeks . . ."

1. John of the Cross, *Sayings of Light and Love*, trans. Kieran Kavanaugh (Washington, DC: ICS Publications, 2005), p. 57.

Go Deeper

REPEAT: "Deliver me, O Lord, from the fear of being humiliated."

PRAY: Consider the criticism of Nathaniel and Jesus's response in John 1:43–5.

READ: *Introduction to the Devout Life* by St. Francis de Sales, Part II, Chapters 26–29.

DO: Don't be defensive when criticism comes your way. Accept it as coming from God as an opportunity to grow in virtue and holiness. Unite your pain to Christ's on the cross.

CHAPTER ELEVEN

Rose: Anger

When you feel the assaults of passion and anger, then is the time to be silent as Jesus was silent in the midst of His ignominies and sufferings.

—St. Paul of the Cross

I was in tears this week before I even made it to church to talk with Fr. Richard. He must have seen it in my eyes and heard it in my voice the moment I entered his office because he said, "Oh, Rose, what's wrong?"

My shoulders trembled as I settled into the chair, the soft glow of sunlight streaming through the stained-glass window casting shadows around me. "He was so angry," I confessed, tears streaming down my cheeks.

Fr. Richard's gentle gaze met mine, his eyes filled with compassion. "Tell me more," he encouraged, his voice a soothing balm to my troubled soul.

"It feels like nearly every day my husband is blowing up about one thing or another. Yesterday, he lost his temper at our son for an assignment he forgot to work on over spring break. I was up late helping him to turn it in on time. The day before that, it was the credit card bill and the extra charges for the summer camps the kids would attend. Last week it was the fact that I drank the last of the coffee without making him more. And today was about how hard he's working and how little I appreciate it. He said some hurtful things in his anger."

Fr. Richard nodded thoughtfully, his brow furrowed with concern as I poured out my heart. "When he gets that angry, do you feel unsafe?" he gently inquired.

I took a moment to collect my thoughts, slightly taken aback by the seriousness of his question. "Do you mean is he violent?" I sought clarification, my voice slightly shaky.

"Yes. With you or the children?" Fr. Richard's concern was palpable, his words laden with empathy.

"No. I honestly can say I've never been afraid he would raise his hand to me in anger. He blows up, yells a lot, and then walks away to cool down. It's uncomfortable and hurtful at the moment, but I'm not afraid of the anger," I explained, feeling a surge of relief. After all, I could admit my husband was a good man.

"That's good! We would never want you, or the children, to be in an unsafe environment," Fr. Richard reassured me gently.

"It's not unsafe, but lately, he seems always angry. In some areas, I think we are making progress—he isn't caught up in work all the time and he no longer hides his phone from me when I walk into the room. Actually, he rarely has his phone on him when at home. It stays in the car many nights. But he comes home from work with this scowl on his face. When I ask if he had a bad day and try to draw him into conversation, he shuts that down pretty quickly. I've stopped asking and checking in, since it never seems to make a difference and he never wants to talk about it."

Fr. Richard nodded thoughtfully, his expression pensive as he processed my words. "You know, people often lash out in anger because they feel unloved or unsafe emotionally. Do you think he might be feeling some of that? Especially if you've stopped reaching out and trying to connect?"

I paused, his words striking a chord within me. "I never considered that, but possibly. Months ago, I would always try to talk with him. Still, after I accused him of having an affair and he denied it, I pretty much stopped trying to have conversations with him beyond the essentials of parenting and family life. I guess, looking back now, it felt easier that way." I felt a pang of regret as I admitted this out loud.

"And perhaps now, after hearing your suspicions of him cheating and then watching you distance yourself, even though he denied it, he's feeling unloved and unwanted. Perhaps his heart has hardened a bit to try to protect himself," Fr. Richard suggested quietly, his words like a gentle breeze stirring the depths of my soul.

"What have I done?" I asked sadly as I realized the results of my actions.

"Nothing you can't undo if you are determined to. Don't be too hard on yourself. We are all victims of original sin, which means we often get it wrong. But first, let's look at how you can respond to his anger, in the moment, since none of this will be an instant fix," Fr. Richard advised compassionately.

As we delved into strategies for navigating my husband's anger, Fr. Richard drew parallels to Christ's own experiences with anger and persecution.

"Remember, there are many points in Jesus's life when he is met with anger from others. Anger over the things he says. Anger over the way he and his disciples live. Anger over the things—the really good things—he did. The Jews attempt to stone him after he says that he and the Father are one. People are upset when he and his disciples pluck ears of grain to eat on the Sabbath. When he cures a man with a withered hand, again on the Sabbath, they don't rejoice at the miracle but are angry that it is done on the wrong day of the week.

"And, of course, during his passion, he is spat upon, beaten, jeered at, and mocked. The angry people of Jerusalem call for him to be crucified, the same people who greet him as a king just a few days before. Imagine how palpable that anger must have been as Christ stood before them and they yelled over and over, 'Crucify him!' The lesson is in how Christ responds to this undeserved anger. He doesn't offer explanations or excuses. He doesn't try to justify himself. He doesn't tell them to calm down, and he doesn't get angry himself. Instead, he reacts precisely as he taught his disciples to respond—he turns the other cheek. He doesn't let anger and resentment build up within him. He speaks out against doing that specifically; 'every one who is angry with his brother shall be liable to judgment'" (Mt 5:22).

Fr. Richard's words offered me solace and perspective, reminding me that even in the face of unjust anger, there was a path forward rooted in love and forgiveness. "So, should I just let him continue to yell at me and the kids? Is that what it means to turn the other cheek?"

"No, you certainly do not need to be the target of his anger. You should have a sincere conversation with him about these angry outbursts and how they make you feel.

Wait for a moment when he isn't yelling, a time when you're alone, never in front of the children, and then point out what's happening in a loving, non-accusatory way. One of the best formulas I've come across for having these challenging talks with a loved one goes like this:

"Begin by saying 'I feel' and then fill in the emotion you are experiencing. Next, offer what he does that makes you feel this way by saying, 'When you . . .' And then you end with, 'So I'd like to ask you to please . . .' and point out the different reaction you'd like to see.

"So, in your case, it might sound a little like this: *I feel* . . . uncomfortable and hurt *when you* . . . have angry outbursts. *So I'd like to ask you to please* . . . not raise your voice in a harsh way at me or the children."

"Hopefully that works, but even if it doesn't, remember Christ's teaching in the Sermon on the Mount when he says, 'Blessed are you when men revile you and persecute you and utter all kinds of evil against you falsely on my account. Rejoice and be glad, for your reward is great in heaven' (Mt 5:11–12). Remember that this marriage is your path to heaven, which might sometimes mean that dealing with his anger is part of that path. The difficult moments, more than the good ones, are the things that will pave your way to heaven, because the trying times are the opportunities you're given to grow in virtue."

"And should I start asking him about his day again?" I asked, my mind racing with the possibilities of how to mend the fractures in our relationship.

"Do you think he felt like you were nagging or badgering him before?"

"Maybe," I admitted, reflecting on past interactions. "I was pretty dogged to get him to talk to me."

"What about instead of badgering him to open up, you start by sharing an observation and offering your support. It could be something like, 'You look like you've had a long day at the office. Thank you for doing that to provide for this family.' Toss in your observation without any accusation or criticism on your part, and offer a compliment or simple embrace."

"I like that idea, and it speaks directly to what we discussed last time, that his greatest fear is failure. If I point out how he succeeds as a father, spouse, and provider, I will speak directly to his greatest needs. It does seem like he is changing a little, but I have so much animosity built up that I tend to see that pain more clearly than his current efforts to get along better," I said, a glimmer of hope flickering within me.

"That is good to hear! This way, too, you'll show him that he is loved and wanted, in case his anger is coming from a place of feeling unloved."

"I don't want him to feel unloved! He is still the best thing in my life; he always has been since the night we met. And he is such an amazing provider, father, and husband. We've gotten so far off track that I just don't think I tell him that enough. I seem irritated with him all the time, which makes it so much easier to see the things he isn't doing, the ways he is falling short, and the areas I want him to improve in. It seems that even the smallest thing irritates me and sets me off, and that's not fair."

Fr. Richard nodded. "But, you can train your mind to start to see the good things first. See all the great things you love about him and focus on those above and beyond the little annoyances. It takes a sustained effort on your part and will take a lot of practice. But it is doable. You can see the positives first and love his failures because they are opportunities for you to keep growing in virtues like patience and fortitude.

"You know Rose, this reminds me of a very pious elderly parishioner that I used to visit regularly. Once when I was visiting her, as she was nearing the end of her life, one of her children asked her if she was excited to meet their father, her deceased husband, when she got to heaven. Her response was remarkable; she hesitated, and then said that over the many years they were married she had grown to love their father's defects and worried that, perfected in heaven, those flaws that she had come to love would no longer be present. How beautiful and profound was her response! *This* Rose is what we should all strive for."

"What a story! I'll start trying to make that mental switch today. Now, what should I focus on over the next two weeks?" I asked, determined to begin anew.

He replied, "Here's what I'm thinking. . ."

Go Deeper

REPEAT: "Where there is injury, let me sow love."

PRAY: Using the passage about Christ not being accepted in his hometown, the place where people knew him well, in Mark 6:1–6.

READ: Part II of *The Hidden Power of Kindness* by Lawrence G. Lovasik.

DO: Smile when you don't want to, turn the other cheek when needed, and compliment your spouse when you have the chance.

CHAPTER TWELVE

John Patrick: Defensiveness

Death and life are in the power of the tongue,
and those who love it will eat its fruits.

—Proverbs 18:21

"Fr. Richard, we've made huge strides in the last two weeks!" I told him, full of excitement about the changes I was seeing taking place in my marriage for the first time in a long time. They were proving to be challenging but so good, too. My heart raced, not from anxiety, but from genuine enthusiasm and hope.

"That's great to hear, John Patrick. What's changed?" Fr. Richard asked as he leaned toward me, his eyes full of genuine interest and warmth.

"I used your formula to start a gentle conversation, and I have to admit I wasn't sure it was going to work, but it did," I said, recalling the anxiety I had felt before starting that conversation. "I pointed out how frustrated I felt when

I would get home from work, and she immediately launched into a litany of all the things that didn't go right for her that day. Then I asked her to hold off on that until after I changed clothes and said hello to the kids, because then I could give her my full attention. She agreed and apologized for always dumping on me as soon as I walked in the door."

"That's amazing," Fr. Richard said, his face lighting up with a smile.

"But Father, it gets even better!" I continued, my excitement bubbling over. "That gentle conversation led to a long conversation about ourselves and our marriage and how we needed professional help to make sure this commitment lasted until death do us part. So, she asked around and found a therapist who came highly recommended by some friends of ours who themselves were in the midst of divorce proceedings and were able to turn it all around for the better. We had our first appointment a few days ago," I said, feeling relief and apprehension as I remembered that session.

"And how did it go?" Fr. Richard asked curiously.

"It was painful. It was more painful than I thought it would be, since it felt like we were dredging up all kinds of hurts and wounds from the past. I felt that most of the problems were her fault. Learning all the things I was doing that hurt her was not enjoyable. In a lot of ways, I realized that I've been a first-class jerk. It's hard for me to concede, but I believe counseling will be so helpful for us as a couple," I admitted, and as I spoke the words aloud I could sense a weight lift off my shoulders.

"That is so good to hear. Count on my prayers during this time for you and your wife," Fr. Richard promised, his eyes conveying a deep sense of compassion and support.

"Thanks, Fr. Richard! We need all the prayers you can spare. But I'm hopeful that this, combined with my meetings for spiritual direction, will be what I need to help our marriage turn the corner," I said, with a newfound sense of determination.

"Absolutely! Our Lord wants us to apply all the spiritual and human means available to find solutions to our problems. We don't have to rely only on prayer for change to occur! St. Augustine famously said, 'Pray as though everything depended on God, work as though everything depended on you.'"[1]

"The one thing I wanted to talk about today is my wife's sudden increased defensiveness. Since going to the therapist, it feels like she is full of excuses for why she acts or reacts a certain way. It seems she believes her reactions are never her fault. In her mind, it is usually my fault, although now she is also blaming the kids and at times even her parents for the way they raised her. It seems now that we are airing out a lot of the dirty laundry of our marriage in therapy, and then talking about our struggles more after each session, she feels the need to explain and justify herself constantly." I felt frustrated and confused.

"This is truly a tale as old as time! Think of Adam and Eve in the garden. Eve takes the forbidden tree's fruit, eats it, and gives it to Adam. When God asks for an explanation, Adam is quick to blame Eve. And Eve, in turn, blames the serpent. No one wants to take ownership of the sin. Neither Adam nor Eve can admit that they freely chose to eat what

---

1. Augustine of Hippo, quoted in Bruce L. Shelley, *Church History in Plain Language* (Nashville: Thomas Nelson, 1995), p. 49.

they were told not to. They try to look better by passing blame. They are doing so to avoid the pain and shame of disobeying God.

"We are no different today, especially when we find ourselves in difficult or trying situations. Defensiveness is often used to avoid pain or mask the shame we feel for what we have done or neglected to do. It's easier to blame another person than take full responsibility for your role in what happened.

"To turn the blame on you, the children, or even more so on her parents, gives her a chance to see herself as more of a victim than the main protagonist of her life. I'm sure in therapy you'll work through a lot of this together, and even perhaps separately, so you can come to a place of ownership and acceptance of your role in how your life and your marriage look now. I wouldn't worry too much about her defensiveness. You will work all that out in counseling. Take joy in the fact that you are both committed to saving your marriage and rekindling your love.

"Sometimes, even when facing the truth head on, it can be tempting to deflect and become defensive. Think of St. Peter during the Last Supper. He is told outright that he will betray Jesus. He knows Jesus is not a liar, not prone to exaggeration, and yet when faced with the reality that is to come, Peter quickly becomes defensive. 'Lord, I am ready to go with you to prison and to death' (Lk 22:33). And we know that a few short hours later, he abandons Jesus upon his arrest and denies him three times.

"Let me ask you a question," Fr. Richard said.

"Shoot," I replied.

"Who is it you have to defend yourself against?"

Thinking this might be a trick question, I tentatively responded, "In general terms, I'd say someone who is a threat, who might be dangerous."

"Correct," he said. "So, now that you got that question right let me ask you a tougher one. Why would your wife need to defend herself against you?"

"Ouch," I said, feeling a sudden sting of realization. "Are you suggesting I'm the problem here? That my wife views me as dangerous?"

"You tell me. When you lose your temper and yell, or get angry and leave the room, does your wife think, 'Now I'm safe, John Patrick is here'—or does her heart say, 'Look out, I'm about to get hurt, I'm not safe here. I better get ready to protect myself'?"

"Hold on here, I'm a really good guy. I work hard to provide for my family, I don't stop at a bar on the way home after work, I play with the kids, and empty the dishwasher. I could go on if you'd like me to!" I declared emphatically, feeling my chest tighten.

"Wait, do I hear a note of defensiveness here?" Fr. Richard said with a wry smile.

"Well, maybe a little," I responded, ashamed and frustrated. "But it would break my heart if my wife saw me as dangerous. I would never hurt her. My job is to protect her and keep her safe."

"Right you are, but realize, John Patrick, your job is not just to keep her physically safe. Even more important is your responsibility to keep her heart emotionally safe and her soul spiritually safe. It sounds like this may be something you need to bring to your prayer."

"I feel like I just got the wind knocked out of me. I will pray about this," I said, a deep sense of humility washing over me.

"That's the spirit. So, for the next two weeks, here's your plan. . ."

Go Deeper

REPEAT: "Help me to have people feel safe when with me."

PRAY: About the betrayal and defensiveness of Adam and Eve. What pain were they trying to avoid by their actions, and how must God have felt? And ask God to open your eyes to ways that you might be making your spouse feel unsafe.

READ: Chapter 4 of *Interior Freedom* by Jacques Philippe.

DO: Show gratitude for what your spouse does for you throughout the week so your spouse feels more secure in your love.

CHAPTER THIRTEEN

Rose: Loneliness

It is better to be alone with God. His friendship will not fail me, nor His counsel, nor His love. In His strength, I will dare and dare and dare until I die.

—St. Joan of Arc

As I stepped into the church, I was heavily burdened by all my worries. The familiar path to Fr. Richard's office felt longer than usual, each step echoing the turmoil in my heart. When I finally entered and settled into my usual chair, I was greeted by Fr. Richard's presence, calm and reassuring as always.

"Rose, how have you been?" he asked, his tone gentle and inviting.

"Oh, Father! I thought things were improving for a time, but now I'm unsure. We had a couple of weeks where things were good. We were talking more, having deep conversations like we hadn't had in years. But now he's pulling away again," I confessed, my voice tinged with frustration.

"He says there is a new project at work that's taking up much of his time and attention outside the office. But it feels like he's opting to pull away rather than get angry. We're back to him just withdrawing again."

Fr. Richard leaned slightly forward, his eyes filled with concern. "And how is that impacting you?" he asked softly.

"To be honest, I feel lonely. Lonely in a way I haven't experienced before in our marriage. After the few good weeks we had, this feels worse than his anger or withdrawal did before. It feels more personal. It feels like I just got a taste of what a good marriage could be, and then it was taken away from me," I admitted, my voice trembling as I tried to hold back the raw emotions welling within.

Fr. Richard nodded understandingly. "And have you talked to him about it?"

"We have had a few conversations about it. We were able to really talk and not yell at one another, but our discussions always ended the same way. He claims work is demanding right now, and I must face this reality for a while. On the other hand, I want him to make more of an effort to be present when he's home," I explained, still frustrated.

"And he's not open to that?" Fr. Richard asked with gentle curiosity.

"No, well, yes. I don't know. He says he's trying. But it doesn't feel that way. He's always on his phone or laptop, answering questions late into the night and early in the morning. He's started bringing his phone to dinner again and not leaving it in his car overnight. And we finally had a date planned for this weekend, but he already canceled because of a client dinner he needs to attend on Friday instead," I recounted, clearly disappointed.

Fr. Richard looked at me empathetically. "And that leaves you feeling unimportant and alone," he stated simply, cutting to the heart of my feelings.

"Exactly! As you suggested, I'm trying to be understanding and see the good in him. He does a great job of providing for us. He works hard so I can stay at home and raise the kids. He works hard so we can send them to the schools we prefer and so that they each will have a college fund. But it's hard to go to bed alone every night and wake up alone nearly every morning. It's hard when he picks work over our plans," I conceded painfully.

Fr. Richard offered a sympathetic smile. "By this point, you probably already know what I will say to you."

I nodded, trying to brace myself. "Align my suffering to that of Christ's on the cross, and keep working on the marriage?" I replied, barely above a whisper.

"Yes, in a nutshell. But you must look at the bigger picture. I want you to remember two things when the feelings of loneliness seem to consume you. First, you can endure because Christ endured loneliness, too. And second, as a beloved child of God, you are never truly alone," he said, his words carrying the weight of wisdom.

"Sorry, Father, but those are easy sentiments to say but harder ones to live," I responded, feeling frustration and resignation.

Fr. Richard nodded, understanding the difficulty of my situation. "I know. Let's dive into each of these truths. It's interesting to consider that in Jesus's public life, there are very few moments in which he is alone. He will sometimes leave his disciples to go and pray, but inevitably, the crowds follow, and he is no longer by himself. But then, in the exact moment when he truly needs those he loves, he is alone!

"The night before his death, he takes Peter, James, and John—his three best friends—to the Garden of Gethsemane. He needs to pray and prepare himself for what's to come, and he asks them to accompany him in prayer. And what do they do? They fall asleep. He wakes them up and asks them again to be with him in this moment of agony. He sweats blood as he anticipates the reality of what's to come, and they fall asleep again, seemingly oblivious to what he's going through.

"Then he is arrested, and they all run away, leaving him alone. Peter follows at a distance but then denies knowing Jesus three times. While Jesus carries his cross, we never hear of him encountering a single one of the apostles; instead, one stranger is forced to help him carry his cross while another stranger wipes the blood and perspiration off his face. In many ways, Christ is all alone.

"And if there was any doubt that he felt that loneliness, we have a record of the few words Jesus said from the cross. One is a line from Psalm 22:1, 'My God, my God, why hast thou forsaken me.' Rose, he knows what you are feeling. He felt it, too! And not just in an abstract way so he could vaguely relate to those who experience loneliness. He felt loneliness on a deep, personal level. The men he poured so much love and affection into for three years, the men handchosen to lead his Church, the men who claimed they were ready to die for him and would never leave—are nowhere to be seen, except young St. John.

"Not to mention, where in the world were all those people he cured and fed and taught? The ten lepers, the man with the withered hand, the centurion whose slave he healed, the man who had been possessed, the five thousand fed from five loaves and two fish, those present at his teaching in the temple—where were they? If they were there, they certainly weren't standing up for him. They weren't helping him get through his final hours on earth.

"So, when this profound loneliness overwhelms you, turn to Our Lord and ask him for the strength, courage, and fortitude to endure. He's 'been there, done that,' as the saying goes.

"There's also another way to look at your suffering. In Colossians 1:24, St. Paul talks about rejoicing in his sufferings and how he completes what is lacking in Christ's afflictions for the sake of the Church. He means our suffering can be united with Christ's suffering on the cross. When we offer our pain, our loneliness, our trials to God, we are participating in Christ's redemptive work. It's a profound way to find meaning and purpose in our suffering, knowing that it's not in vain but has a spiritual value that contributes to the salvation of souls."

I took a deep breath, letting his words sink in. "I've never thought about how alone Christ was on the cross. I've always pictured the scene more from the perspective of him looking down on his mother Mary, John, and Mary Magdalene, who were there at the time."

"Yes, and surely they were a consolation for him. But think of it like this: you have your children, your friends, and some family, and yet when your husband is missing, you are lonely for him. I'm sure Jesus felt the same. He was probably so grateful for those present at the foot of the cross while also feeling acutely saddened over those who were missing," Fr. Richard explained, his voice filled with empathy.

"It's true. I always feel a little guilty when I feel lonely, even when the kids are around. Like, they should be enough to fill that void," I admitted remorsefully.

"But they can't fill the space a husband is supposed to occupy. Your children and friends can help you get outside of yourself and you can pour yourself out in loving and serving them. But it's OK to acknowledge that they—as great as they are—are not the same as your husband," Fr. Richard explained with kind understanding.

"They aren't!" I agreed, feeling a bit lighter as he validated my feelings.

"I've given you a lot to think about already, but I want to make sure we touch on my second point for you to consider when loneliness descends upon you. You are a child of God, a beloved daughter. This is the most profound reality of your identity and existence. Christ made all of this possible through that lonely passion and death of his. He truly made us his brothers and sisters, children of God the Father.

"And just like any perfect father, God is always there for you! He's by your side, lifting you and holding you in the palm of his hand. He's not some distant God who can't be bothered with the creatures he made. He's not some genie in a bottle, waiting to grant us wishes when we pray. No! He's a father. A father who is willing to give the very best to his children.

"Do you remember the story of the Prodigal Son?"

"That's the story of the man with two sons—one who stayed with him and one who took his inheritance and left, right?" I asked, somewhat familiar with the tale.

"Exactly! The father in that story offers us a small glimpse into the love that God the Father has for us. If you pay attention to the details of that story, you will find that the specifics are very moving. When the younger son, who took the money and ran, returns home, he doesn't have to knock on his father's door to let him know he has arrived. There isn't a servant who goes and informs his father either. St. Luke says, 'But while [the son] was yet at a distance, his father saw him and had compassion, and ran and embraced him and kissed him' (Lk 15:20). The father looked down the road and waited for his son to come home. How many times must he have done this? When the father sees him, despite his son's haggard appearance from the life he had been living, the father recognizes him immediately. He runs and embraces him. He embraces this smelly son of his who had left him without a backward glance. He embraces his son who lived an unclean, sinful, life. He is clearly overjoyed to have him back again.

"God the Father is the same way with us. He is always there, always looking down the road, always ready with a warm embrace and a kiss. You are not alone—even in the darkest moments of your life and your marriage. God is there, and he will never leave you. He will always be like the father of the prodigal son!"

I wiped a few tears from my eyes before saying, "I've never pictured God like that, but it fills me with hope."

"It's a great passage to take to your prayer and to reflect upon as you consider what it means to have a Father who loves you that much."

"I think I already know that part of my assignment these next two weeks will be to pray about Christ's loneliness on the cross and about my God as my loving Father. I do think that will help give me a better perspective concerning my loneliness as my husband is swept up in this new project."

"Good, good! Lastly, I'd say personally, whenever I feel loneliness begin to creep in, I try to push myself to think of others and serve them instead of wallowing in my thoughts and emotions. It often helps to spend time with a friend or volunteer to help those in need. Getting outside of ourselves can help give us a more complete picture of our lives and the many gifts we have but often take for granted."

"I have a few friends I haven't seen in ages. I can plan to meet up with them for coffee or lunch."

"Do that! And Rose, while this is hard, I have to say there seems to be some great progress in your marriage and in your heart. Be sure to thank God for that!"

"It's true. Sometimes, I get so caught up in what isn't right that I forget to look and see all the good around me and all the progress that has been made. We are truly communicating for the first time in years. We are both trying to improve and work on our marriage and ourselves." A sense of calm washed over me as I admitted this. The path ahead still seemed challenging, but Fr. Richard's words had given me new strength and perspective. I felt ready to face the days ahead, buoyed by the knowledge that I was not alone in this journey.

"There is a lot to give thanks for! Here's your work for the weeks ahead: Pray on these truths, reach out to your friends, and keep communicating with your husband. I'll be praying for you both." And he jotted the assignment down. . .

Go Deeper

REPEAT: "Deliver me, O Lord, from the fear of being forgotten."

PRAY: Meditate on Psalms 22 and 31.

READ: Chapter 1 of *The Sadness of Christ* by St. Thomas More.

DO: Pour yourself into others, plan a date night to reconnect with your spouse, reach out to a friend, write a love letter to Jesus.

CHAPTER FOURTEEN

John Patrick: Contempt

When you are insulted by someone or humiliated, guard against angry thoughts, lest they arouse a feeling of irritation, and so cut you off from love and place you in the realm of hatred.

—St. Maximos the Confessor

John Patrick, how has marriage therapy been going?" Fr. Richard asked as soon as I settled into my chair, his eyes filled with concern and curiosity.

I chuckled a little at the question. "I didn't realize things would get worse before they got better when we started seeing a therapist. I guess I naively thought things were at their lowest, and we could only improve from there," I said, shaking my head at my earlier ignorance.

"And that's not the case?" Fr. Richard leaned in, his brows furrowing slightly.

"Therapy is hard. We are digging into a lot of old, deep wounds and persistent patterns that have been hurting us individually and as a couple. It's not been easy to see all the ways I've contributed to these issues, and it's been even harder hearing directly from my wife all the ways I've caused her pain," I admitted, feeling a knot form in my stomach as the words left my mouth.

"But is it worth it?" Fr. Richard asked, his voice gentle and understanding.

"Yes! We're talking for the first time in years. We can say things to one another—hard things—lovingly, building a deeper connection rather than creating a greater divide. It's just been a lot, and it's pretty overwhelming! I'm constantly lost in my thoughts now, analyzing what we talked about at our last therapy session and what I've learned about her and myself in the process. It's challenging," I stated, feeling relief and exhaustion.

"I'm glad to hear it's helping and that you are both leaning into the process," Fr. Richard said with a hint of pride in his voice.

As I felt a wave of guilt wash over me, I confessed, "I think what's hard is that we're still defensive about some of the things that are brought up in our therapy sessions, blaming it on others and making ourselves seem like the victim in all of this. When our anger shows up, we can say some pretty hurtful things about each other, our parents, or whoever's in the narrative."

"Contempt is a common issue in many marriages. I imagine that as you are working through a lot of this, it will be difficult at times to accept what you're hearing. As we talked about last time, it's easier to blame others at times than to peel back our protective layers and see the corruption that lies there," Fr. Richard said, knowingly but empathetically.

"True. Because we are dredging up so much from our past, it seems like these memories from previous pain are fresh again, and when I get angry, she reacts strongly. In the past, she had never said much about it. But now, in therapy and even when we are home after a session, she has started saying some mean things when she's upset. The other day, she compared me to her brothers. One's a lawyer, and the other owns his own super-successful business, and of course, the comparison makes me feel like a bum who doesn't make enough money for the kind of summer vacation she'd like to take. I make good money, but we allocate it differently than her single brothers do. I made the mistake of defending myself by pointing out all our extra responsibilities as parents. Then, suddenly, I was a 'senseless idiot,'" I recounted, feeling the sting of those words anew.

"That can't be easy to hear, even if you can acknowledge that this is all part of the process you are going through, as a couple, to work things out. It sounds like you know she isn't intending to lash out at you in that way," Fr. Richard observed quietly.

"I don't think she even realizes she's doing it. The words and comparisons come out in the heat of the moment, and then it blows over just as quickly," I said. Recalling these episodes left me feeling frustrated and sad.

Fr. Richard gazed at me steadily and asked, "And how do you respond?"

"Lately, I'm trying to get less angry, so often I end up just walking away from her and pouring myself into work," I admitted, ashamed.

"Which isn't a solution either, is it?" Fr. Richard pointed out gently.

"I know, I know. It's just the easiest option at the time," I said, feeling the weight of my shortcomings.

"It sounds like you need to talk about the growing hostility you are showing each other. Maybe you can discuss this with the therapist," Fr. Richard suggested.

"Absolutely!" I agreed, nodding vigorously.

"I'll let the therapist handle that side of the equation. I'm here to give you the spiritual dimension, since that's my area of expertise. Facing hurtful speech is nothing new. We see it many times in the Bible—both in the Old and New Testaments. A few situations that come quickly to mind would be when the Israelites say horrible things about Moses and the land he led them to, despite the fact that he saved them from slavery and was taking them to the Promised Land of milk and honey; or when Job's friends were convinced he must have done something wrong for God to be punishing him with the loss of his family and fortune; another might be when Noah was mocked for building the ark and warning the people to repent before it was too late. Even the early Christians experienced Saul's 'murderous threats,' and I'm sure there are many more such examples.

"All of these people who experienced contempt didn't retaliate. Most of them didn't even offer an explanation or try to justify their behavior. Instead, they used this mean speech to strengthen their resolve to do the right thing. The early Christians, in the face of persecution and death, didn't cower. Rather, they continued to spread the faith, so that three hundred years after the death of Christ, Christianity was named the state religion of the Roman Empire.

"You can do the same. Use the contempt you're experiencing from your wife to strengthen your resolve to fix your marriage and to be the best husband and father you can be. You can use her words to align yourself with Our Lord when he suffered the ridiculing during his passion. This approach will help you grow closer to the man he calls you to be. Otherwise, you will use those words to become bitter and resentful. My advice is to use them for good.

"Remember, your wife is your path to heaven! So, her failings, flaws, and faults are a chance for you to grow in virtue. In this scenario, it's a chance for you to grow in patience, perseverance, and charity. Don't squander this opportunity that God is giving you to become better! Like him, you can take evil and turn it into good just by how you react," Fr. Richard said, challenging and inspiring me.

"It's hard to remember in the heat of the moment, when she is upset and unkind because of some previous pain, that this is my path to heaven. It certainly doesn't feel like it," I admitted helplessly.

"Of course it doesn't. But iron is forged in fire. You're being forged into a new man as you go through this. What that man looks like is largely based on how you approach and address these situations," Fr. Richard said, his voice firm yet gentle.

"It certainly feels like a forge at times," I muttered, a small smile playing on my lips despite the seriousness of the conversation.

"It's bound to feel like that. A life aligned with God and his will is not meant to be one without challenges and difficulties, but Jesus does promise that when we take up his yoke, it will be easy and light. But in order to do that, we must leave our heavy burden at his feet. I read somewhere that in Jesus's time, each yoke had to be custom-built for each ox. If it wasn't tailored precisely, it would cause the ox to develop a sore and then the poor beast wouldn't pull the plow. Guess who made the yokes in Jesus's time? Yep, the carpenters. So, Jesus would have had real experience crafting precise yokes. Therefore, when he says, 'My yoke is easy,' he knows what he's talking about. You can't carry both the yoke you've fashioned and the one God has made for you. Cast off the yoke you've constructed for yourself and embrace the one Jesus has fitted to you," Fr. Richard explained, his words painting a vivid picture.

"This yoke doesn't feel all that light right now," I said, feeling the weight of my struggles.

"That's because you need to get better at letting go and letting God. Think of when Our Lord suffered the crowning with thorns! This is after he's already been scourged. His body is a bloody mess, and the soldiers wrap him in a dirty purple robe and put a crown of thorns on his head. They hit him and spit on him. This is a mockery of him as a king and only a tiny portion of what he will experience during the coming hours.

"And yet he endures! How? Science can't explain how any man could have survived all he went through before even being nailed to the cross. But he does endure, because this is the will of the Father. Because this was the price he agreed to pay for our redemption. Because this was the plan for his life—as difficult and painful as that would be.

"We are no different. Not only can we survive, but we can become saints by aligning our will with the will of God and using every painful moment to bring us closer to him. Your wife's contempt right now as you work through things in therapy is your current cross. It is the sacrifice God is asking you to endure so that you and your wife can be better, holier people.

"St. Josemaría said in his book *Holy Rosary*, 'Don't bear your Cross with resignation: resignation is not a generous word. Love the Cross. When you love it, your Cross will be . . . a Cross, without a Cross.'[1] But you need to bear it squarely on your shoulders, take it on, and be ready to do what needs to be done for her, for you, for your marriage, and for your children," Fr. Richard said, his words resonating deeply within me.

"I like it. It feels like the manly way to approach this." I felt a renewed sense of determination.

"It is that, but it's also the childish way to approach this. Childish as in a child of God, who wants to please his Father more than anything in the world," Fr. Richard said, his eyes twinkling.

"The childish way," I nodded. "I might like that even more."

"That's the reality. We are nothing but small children before our loving Father. I know how much your father meant to you and how much love he gave you as you were growing up. God as a Father is ten thousand times better than that! Here's what I think you can focus on for the next two weeks . . ."

---

1. Josemaría Escrivá, *Holy Rosary* (New York: Scepter, 1989), p. 31.

Go Deeper

REPEAT: "Help me to accept being humiliated as a gift."

PRAY: Meditate on Job's innocence despite his friends' contempt.

READ: Book of Job, chapters 8–9.

DO: Make excuses for your spouse's behavior by putting yourself in her shoes. Root out any mean speech from your own life.

CHAPTER FIFTEEN

Rose: Eight Months Later

Love should be seen as something which in a sense never 'is' but is always only 'becoming,' and what it becomes depends upon the contribution of both persons and the depth of their commitment.

—St. John Paul II

Hand in hand, my husband and I walked up the church steps on a beautiful spring morning. If someone had told me a year ago, when I first sought Fr. Richard's help in spiritual direction, that my husband and I would be more in love today than ever before, I would have laughed in utter disbelief. At the time, I felt like we were one fight away from divorce, and I honestly doubted whether I would ever be happy again. How could I, when so much seemed wrong in my life?

But God works in mysterious ways. His grace led me to the confessional that day many months ago and prompted me to ask for guidance from a priest I barely knew outside of the sacrament. That one moment of grace, and no doubt the millions that followed after, completely changed my life and my marriage.

"Are you ready for this?" John Patrick asked, holding the door open so I could precede him inside.

"So ready," I responded with a smile, squeezing his arm lightly as I walked by. "He's going to be thrilled."

Fr. Richard was waiting for us in a sitting room off the narthex. When we walked in, he stood up with a large smile on his face and his hand outstretched to shake ours.

"Rose, John Patrick, it's so good to see the two of you together!"

"We wanted to tell you something but couldn't decide who should be the one to tell you, so we decided it was best if we both came this time," I told him while sitting on the couch. John Patrick sat down next to me, his arm going along the back of the sofa, his hand resting on my back. A year ago, this simple gesture would have never happened. Now, it happens all the time.

"Tell me, tell me," Fr. Richard encouraged, a wide grin spreading across his face.

"Rose is expecting!" John Patrick blurted out, unable to contain his excitement.

"God is good!" Father responded instantly. We both nodded in agreement.

"I'm having a boy, and we want to name him Richard after you," I said, seeking his approval.

"Without your guidance, I don't think we'd be together today, and certainly, our fourth child would not be on the way if it weren't for you," my husband told him sincerely. We credited this child to the wisdom that Fr. Richard shared and the encouragement he gave us to endure the suffering in our marriage while looking for ways to improve it.

I placed my hand on John Patrick's knee and continued, "We've said it before, but it bears repeating: we are so grateful for all you did."

Fr. Richard shook his head, humble as ever. "Not me. God worked the miracle while the two of you put in the work. I simply suggested new ways to look at the situation and topics for your prayer."

"It was so much more than that," my husband argued. "You taught me about the redemptive value of suffering. The pain I was going through could be aligned to Christ's cross, and good could come from it."

"And you taught me that to be a saint in the world today, this guy," I squeezed John Patrick's knee for emphasis, "is my path. My only path to heaven. John Patrick, with all his strengths and weaknesses, is going to help me reach heaven one day."

"That's true! But I think I offered you both more a reminder of the truths you already knew," Fr. Richard insisted.

"No. You changed my entire mindset, my perspective about suffering and its meaning. Before we started talking, I thought the pain I experienced in my marriage was a punishment from God and useless. But now I know we can't escape suffering in this life, but we can use it to grow holier and happier. Now I stub my toe and am almost thankful for the moment of pain. Almost," John Patrick said with a shrug.

We both still had a long way to go in understanding and accepting suffering, but we were on a great path.

"I must tell you, I read and pray with the scriptures differently now. I see many instances in which Jesus can relate to whatever I feel at a given moment. The other day, I wasn't feeling great, battling a little morning sickness, so I tried to leave the kids with John Patrick so I could get a nap. But the kids wanted to be with me, and soon, they ran around the room, jumping on the bed, and did not give me a minute of peace. I was frustrated, but then I remembered that passage where Jesus escaped to pray alone, and the children came. The apostles tried to chase them away, but Jesus allowed the kids to disrupt his prayer and said, 'Let the children come' (Lk 18:16). I just kept repeating that aspiration over and over again that day when I found myself overwhelmed."

"That's beautiful," Fr. Richard said. "Christ was the perfect God and perfect man, so he has a lot to teach us if we open our eyes to the Scriptures in a new way. We don't have to read the passages the same way we always have—the gospel is ever new."

"Plus, you suggested we try a marriage therapist—something I never considered before and once believed needing one was a sign that I was a failure. But I now think it's the second-best thing we did for our marriage—the first best thing was getting spiritual direction from you," I told him.

Fr. Richard grinned. "God puts both the supernatural and human means at our disposal for a reason. Sometimes it's best to use them together," he agreed.

"I'm so glad we got over that fear and decided to take a leap of faith and get into therapy," I continued, thinking back to those first few weeks and how much more difficult it made our marriage before making it infinitely better. In those initial sessions, I questioned whether it was a mistake and if we had somehow managed to make it even worse. It took some time, a lot of deep conversations, and a lot of exposed raw emotions to begin to heal ourselves and our marriage.

"Even our kids have noticed a difference," John Patrick told him. "I thought they were clueless as to what was going on between the two of us. But last week, I cleaned the garage with our oldest son, and he said, 'Dad, I'm glad you love Mom again.' That hit me hard, and I choked up a little. But I told him honestly, 'I never stopped loving your mom, but for a while, we had a hard time showing each other that love.'"

"The children always see more than they let on," Father said.

"It got me thinking that I want to be a great example to him of what a husband should be so that when it's his turn to get married, he'll have a blueprint for how to treat his wife, how to love her well, how to put her first, and even, at times, how to suffer well."

Fr. Richard wiped a small tear from the corner of his eye, smiling at the two of us. "I have no doubt he'll understand well if you keep pursuing sanctity together."

"We plan to," my husband said confidently.

"I want to remind you both that while this is like a new honeymoon period in your marriage, this does not mean there won't be future suffering to endure. I've yet to meet a married couple that doesn't suffer, that doesn't at times hurt one another. And you won't be that exception. Suffering is a part of life. Remember, Our Lord didn't even spare his mother or himself the suffering that was his passion and death. But it becomes much easier to endure when we have our eyes fixed on heaven and remember the goal and path God has marked out for us. As St. Paul reminded the Philippians, 'I can do all things in him who strengthens me'" (Phil 4:13).

I smiled at Fr. Richard's wisdom, feeling profound gratitude for his guidance. As we left the church, hand in hand, I reflected on how far we had come. This new chapter in our lives felt like a blessing, a renewal, and a promise of more incredible things to come.

Eight months earlier, I had walked into the narthex on an ordinary day, needing to ask Fr. Richard some questions, even though it wasn't my scheduled appointment time or day. The door to his office was closed, but the light was on. I decided to wait, taking a seat just outside. A few minutes later, the door opened, and my heart stopped as John Patrick walked out. My mind raced with confusion and surprise.

"What are you doing here?" I asked, my voice tinged with disbelief.

He looked as confused as I felt. "What am I doing here? What are you doing here?"

"I asked you first," I retorted, struggling to process the whirlwind of emotions—anger, sadness, maybe even happiness.

John Patrick replied, "I meet Fr. Richard every other week for spiritual direction now."

Still reeling, I said, "Wait, you see Fr. Richard for spiritual direction? He's my spiritual director. I also see him every other week for spiritual direction."

Fr. Richard, who stood in the doorway looking both amused and concerned, stepped into the hallway. "So, neither of you knew the other one was coming to me for spiritual direction? Why don't you both come in and sit down."

As we sat, I asked John Patrick how long he had been seeing Fr. Richard.

"For about four months," he admitted. "My life was so out of control. You and I were fighting all the time. I was angry and scared that our marriage was failing, and we were going to be one of those statistics, just one more divorce among thousands. I didn't know what to do or where to turn. I used to see Fr. Richard for direction before we were married, so I looked him up and scheduled an appointment. But you, how do you know Fr. Richard?"

"I didn't know him. One day, I was just driving past the church and felt an overwhelming desire to go to confession. You and I had just had another big fight, and I was desperate to talk to someone. Fr. Richard was in the confessional that day, and he suggested I begin receiving spiritual direction from him. I agreed. This was entirely a Holy Spirit thing."

"I don't know what to say," John Patrick continued. "I knew I had to do a lot of work on myself. I was so angry and blamed you for our problems. I knew that wasn't true, but I was in such a dark place that I couldn't see the truth. Fr. Richard enlightened me to how I was hurting you and what a knucklehead I had been. Most of our problems were because of me, not you. I have not been a good husband or friend to you. I did not protect your heart; quite the contrary, I became very dangerous to your heart and happiness. I am so sorry."

I reached over and held his hand. "No, that's not true. I have not been the wife I should have been. I was so quick to criticize and blame you. I hurt you so many times with the cruel and mean things I said. But I was in a dark place as well. I was so confused and scared. I loved you so much when we got married. I couldn't believe that I was carrying so much anger around with me. Fr. Richard worked his magic on me as well. I am as much to blame as you are for our troubles."

I recall that when I looked up at John Patrick and I saw his beautiful eyes brimming with tears, I started crying like I hadn't cried in a long time. He pulled me close and put his forehead on my shoulder. We didn't talk for a long time. Then he said softly, "I love you and will make this right. I will become the husband you deserve. I will protect your heart, and I will never again do anything to hurt you."

I hadn't felt so warm, loved, or safe in my life. I turned and kissed him on the cheek and said, "Love you more," which was a phrase we used to say to each other when we were first married. He started to laugh, and I began to cry even more.

As I began to dry my tears, I said, "Fr. Richard, you must think we're pretty weird." But as I looked around, I realized his office was empty except for John Patrick and me. This remarkable priest had managed to slip out of the room without us noticing. Thank God for holy priests. We finally pulled ourselves together, but I didn't want to let go of my newfound husband. I wrapped my arms tightly around him as he walked me to my car. Then he climbed into the passenger side, and we continued to talk until it was time to pick the kids up from school. He decided to take the rest of the day off from work. That was the day we launched our marriage 2.0.

Reflecting on all this while sitting with Fr. Richard today, I realized how pivotal that moment was for us. It set the stage for the growth and healing we experienced over the next eight months. And now, with a new baby on the way and a renewed sense of love and commitment, I couldn't be more grateful for the journey we undertook together.

And of course, as we were leaving today, Fr. Richard gave us one more assignment that we could work on together . . .

Go Deeper

REPEAT: "Lord, help me to love you through loving my spouse."

PRAY: Using Pope Francis's *Amoris Laetitia,* Chapter 4.

READ: *Catechism of the Catholic Church,* Section on Man, nos. 355–384.

DO: Make a fifteen-minute investment in your marriage daily! This means having a one-on-one conversation, without the kids and without using it as a planning session, to focus on your relationship.

Recommended Reading

Catechism of the Catholic Church, 2nd ed. 2019. Vatican City: Libreria Editrice Vaticana.
Read Paragraph 6. "Man," nos. 355–384.

Escrivá, Josemaría. 1997. *Friends of God*. New York: Scepter.
Read the homily "Toward Holiness."

Faus, Francesc. 2011. *A Man Who Knew How to Forgive: Incidents from the Life of St. Josemaría Escrivá*. New York: Scepter.

Francis, Pope. 2016. Post-Synodal Apostolic Exhortation *Amoris Laetitia*. www.vatican.va.
Read Chapter 4.

Liguori, Alphonsus de. *The Glories of Mary*.
Read Discourse 9, "Of the Dolors of Mary."

Lovasik, Lawrence G. 1999. *The Hidden Power of Kindness: A Practical Handbook for Souls Who Dare to Transform the World, One Deed at a Time.* Manchester, NH: Sophia Institute Press.
Read Part II.

More, Thomas. (1993.) *The Sadness of Christ.* New York: Scepter.
Read Chapter 1.

Philippe, Jacques. 2002. *Searching for and Maintaining Peace.* New York: Alba House.

———. 2007. *Interior Freedom.* New York: Scepter.
Read Chapter 4.

Resurrection, Lawrence of the. *The Practice of the Presence of God.*

Saint-Jure, Jean Baptiste, and Claude de la Colombiere. 1980. *Trustful Surrender to Divine Providence: The Secret of Peace and Happiness.* Rockford, IL: Tan Books.

Sales, Francis de. *Introduction to the Devout Life.*
Read Part II, Chapters 26–29.

Ugarte, Francisco. 2008. *From Resentment to Forgiveness: A Gateway to Happiness.* New York: Scepter.
Read Chapter 1 and Chapter 4.